W9-CLY-372

THE
Suicidal
Mind

THE
Suicidal
Mind

Edwin S. Shneidman

OXFORD UNIVERSITY PRESS
New York   Oxford

Oxford University Press

Oxford   New York
Athens   Auckland   Bangkok   Bogotá   Bombay
Buenos Aires   Calcutta   Cape Town   Dar es Salaam
Delhi   Florence   Hong Kong   Istanbul   Karachi
Kuala Lumpur   Madras   Madrid   Melbourne
Mexico City   Nairobi   Paris   Singapore
Taipei   Tokyo   Toronto   Warsaw

and associated companies in
Berlin   Ibadan

Copyright © 1996 by Edwin S. Shneidman

First published by Oxford University Press, Inc., 1996
First issued as an Oxford University Press paperback, 1998

Oxford is a registered trademark of Oxford University Press

All rights reserved. No part of this publication may be reproduced,
stored in a retrieval system, or transmitted, in any form or by any means,
electronic, mechanical, photocopying, recording, or otherwise,
without the prior permission of Oxford University Press.

Library of Congress Cataloging-in-Publication Data
Shneidman, Edwin, 1918–
The suicidal mind / Edwin Shneidman.
p.   cm. Includes index.

ISBN-13 978-0-19-511801-8

1. Suicidal behavior.   I. Title.
RC569.S385   1996   616.85'8445—dc20   95–42071

20 19 18 17 16 15 14
Printed in the United States of America

Again,

To the Shining Memory of

HENRY A. MURRAY

who taught me that life,

more vast than I had imagined,

was a wondrous process of discovery,

and that death,

while it might be explored,

can never be fully charted

PREFACE

It has been a hundred years since the pioneer French sociologist Emile Durkheim wrote *Le Suicide*. The past century has seen intellectual, social, as well as political changes. Many basic customs around death and dying have been radically altered; our understandings of suicide have been changed and mutated. Two disciplines, central to suicidology, were at their beginnings when Durkheim wrote his influential book near the turn of the century. In Europe, Freud had just begun to publish and, in America, William James had written his monumental *Principles of Psychology* just a few years before. Of the two new disciplines, psychology remained remote from practical issues like suicide prevention, whereas psychiatry tried to medicalize suicide. Both lost the essence of suicide—one to irrelevant experimentation, and the other to Kraepelin's typology (seen today in the *Diagnostic and Statistical Manual*). Neither psychology nor psychiatry can be counted as grand successes as far as suicide is concerned.

This book is a forthright effort to revitalize the topic of suicide by looking in a fresh way at suicidal phenomena as they play themselves out in the minds of suicidal people.

The central lesson of this book is that the keys to understanding suicide are made of plain language; that the proper language of suicidology is *lingua franca*—the ordinary everyday words that are found in the verbatim reports of beleaguered suicidal minds.

It is the words that suicidal people say—about their psychological pain and their frustrated psychological needs—that make up the essential vocabulary of suicide. Suicide prevention can be everybody's business.

The clinical core of the book lies in the case histories. Three electrifying cases of fatally intended suicide attempts illustrate why people kill themselves. There is Ariel, a woman who set herself on fire; Beatrice, an adolescent who cut herself with the intent to die; and Castro, a young man who meant to shoot his brains out, but, instead, blew his face off. These unforgettable cases—presented in the person's own words—allow the reader to view the workings of the suicidal mind, to see its most dangerous moments.

Although this book is necessarily about pain, I hope that it will not be a painful experience to read it. For me, writing this book has been exciting and personally insightful, and I fret over it, as I have fretted over all my offspring. I have saved for the Acknowledgments the names of those special people who have helped me convert my gossamer fantasy of this volume into a tangible reality. The principal goals of all my writing on suicide for the past 45 years have been to be helpful and to relieve pain. I live with the hope that I am not deluded in this aspiration.

E. S.

Los Angeles
February 1996

ACKNOWLEDGMENTS

Grateful acknowledgment is made for permission to reprint:

Extended excerpts from the writings of Henry A. Murray. Permission given by Dr. Caroline F. Murray of Nantucket.

Abstracts from the Terman Study of the Gifted. Permission given by Professor Albert Hastorf of Stanford University, scientific executor of the Terman Study.

The McGill Pain Questionnaire from *The Handbook of Pain Assessment*, edited by D. C. Turk and R. Melzack, published by Guilford Press, 1992. Permission granted by Guilford Press.

Excerpt from "An Interior Pain that Is All but Indescribable" by William Styron, from *Newsweek*, April 18, 1994. Copyright 1994 by Newsweek, Inc. All rights reserved. Reprinted by permission.

Paragraph from *Buddenbrooks* by Thomas Mann, translated by H. T. Lowe-Porter. Copyright 1924 and renewed 1952 by Alfred A. Knopf, Inc. Copyright 1964 by Alfred A. Knopf, Inc. Reprinted by permission of the publisher.

Selections from "Directions to the Armorer" by Elder Olson.

New Yorker, November 14, 1959. Copyright 1959, 1987. All rights reserved. Reprinted by permission.

And now for some other happy debts I am glad to pay. I wish to thank:

My Los Angeles neighbors, Roz and Si Bessen and Maureen and Mort Bernstein, who stood in for the everyman reader to whom this book is addressed; Nancy H. Allen, M. P. H., my longtime and treasured colleague at NIMH and UCLA; Shirley Zimmerman, Ph.D., my special friend at the University of Minnesota; Robert E. Litman, M.D., UCLA, my colleague and friend of a lifetime; John T. Maltsberger, M.D., McLean Hospital and Harvard Medical School, voice of reason and affection; Caroline (Nina) Murray, Ed.D., my beloved friend and Henry Murray's widow; Robert O. Pasnau, M.D., UCLA, who helped me with the three cases central to this book; Fawzi I. Fawzi, M.D., UCLA, who helped this project with space, administrative support, and pleasant ambience; Antoon Leenaars, Ph.D., Windsor, Ontario, Canada, simultaneous student and teacher; Albert Hastorf, Ph.D., and Eleanor Walker, Terman Study at Stanford University, who, for years, encouraged one major aspect of my lifetime work; Mamoru Iga, Ph.D., Northridge, California, who gave me valuable insights into another culture; Yoshitomo Takahashi, M.D., Tokyo Psychiatric Institute, who clued me in on the voice of contemporary Japanese psychiatry.

My nine "mess-mates" of our weekly emeritus luncheon group at UCLA, now in its tenth year: Benjamin Aaron, J.D. (law); Irving Bernstein, Ph.D. (Political Science); Lester Breslow, M.D. (Public Health): Alma Hawkins (Dance); Hal Horowitz, J.D. (Law); Fredrick Redlich, M.D. (Psychiatry); David Saxon, Ph.D. (Physics); Murray

Schwartz, J.D. (Law); and Harry Wasserman, Ph.D. (Social Welfare).

Regina Ryan of New York City, my nonpareil agent, always the voice of reason, always the advice of prudence; Joan Bossert, perspicacious editor of Oxford University Press, patron saint of the beautiful arts, who initiated this project, and showed me how a first-rate editor can improve every aspect of a latent manuscript; and Rosemary Wellner, eagle-eyed book-carver in the hinterlands of New Hampshire.

Jeanne K. Shneidman, my soul mate for over half a century in our marriage of hearts and minds, who has helped me in everything and enriched everything she touched.

CONTENTS

PART IV   Staying Alive

DISPUTATION

I remember times when the inner disputation
Was quite fierce (to pursue the game, or sign
A full stop to pain). The call was mine—
Or so it seemed. Each voice a singular temptation:

The beguiling cries of longed-for rest,
The easeful quiet, the total peace
—what a boon!—finally to cease
The struggle; to know that nothingness is best.

But then, from the barely bubbling sieve
Of my active self, a tired but urgent call
To return to habit and duty; reluctantly to fall
Again into pain and heartache—and to live.

Oh soul! thou then stood on an isthmus break
And heard, in separate ears, Aegean and Ionian wave.
Which sea? To drown, or combers once again to brave?
The vital choice was solely mine to make.

PART ONE

The Dark Side of Life

1

Why Do We Kill Ourselves?

Suicide haunts our literature and our culture. It is the taboo subtext to our successes and our happiness. The reporting of a suicide of any public figure disturbs each of us. Amid our dreams of happiness and achievement lurk our nightmares of self-destruction. Who is not mindful of the potential self-defeating elements within our own personality? Each new day contains the threat of failure and assaults by others, but it is the threat of *self*-destruction that we are most afraid to touch, except in our secret moments or the hidden recesses of our minds. Yet suicide happens every day, and many people we know have had a relative or a friend who has committed suicide.

I got into suicide quite by accident. It was in 1949; I was 31. On that particular morning, I was in the subbasement, below the street level of the old Los Angeles Hall of Records, in the Coroner's vault, looking at file-folders of certified deaths. I had been asked by the Director of the Veterans Administration hospital where I worked as a clinical psychologist to prepare letters to be sent to two young widows whose husbands had committed suicide while they were still wards of the hospital. My intention that day was to look at the folders of the two men, make some notes, and get back to work.

The first folder contained something I had not seen before: a suicide note; the second folder did not. Who could stop at this point? I looked at several dozen folders. It seemed that every so often I would open a suicide folder and find a suicide note—about 1 in 15. I did a quick count of the number of the folders on one shelf and I estimated that I was in a room that contained at least a couple thousand suicide notes. It was a scientist's dream. Within the next few weeks I made photocopies of over 700 suicide notes and put them aside, without reading them, later to be compared in "blind," controlled studies with simulated suicide notes elicited from nonsuicidal people. Since that day, I have been intrigued by the topic of suicide and drawn to people who might be suicidal.

What is suicide anyway? How can we understand it and prevent it? This book has a definite point of view. Stripped down to its bones, my argument goes like this: In almost every case, suicide is caused by pain, a certain kind of pain—*psychological* pain, which I call *psychache* (sīk-āk). Furthermore, this psychache stems from thwarted or distorted psychological *needs*. In other words, suicide is chiefly a drama in the mind. This book is about the suicidal mind.

My statement about the root cause of suicide is an assertion that comes from my half-century of experience with suicidal individuals across the country. When I say that almost all suicide is caused by psychache, exactly how much suicide do I believe is so motivated? All?—Not quite. Most?—Certainly. Are there exceptions?—No doubt. Is this notion intended to apply equally to such events as hara-kiri, seppuku, suttee, or acts of suicidal terrorists?—No. I make no attempt to cover suicide in cultures different from our own Judeo-Christian tradition, explicitly not suicides in China or India or Islam, where special historical and cultural forces are sufficiently powerful that people are willing to die for them. This topic is a very complicated business. Some suicidal acts committed by people on what we call "suicide missions" or who commit aberrant acts of terrorism are, when done by *our* side (in times of war), honored and rewarded by medals. Indeed, the Congressional Medal of Honor is awarded for brave actions that, by any normal calculations, would have resulted in death—and sometimes did. But wartime heroism and rare sacrificial suicides aside, this book is primarily intended for an American and European readership and is meant to address directly the state of the suicidal mind.

Even though I know that each suicidal death is a multifaceted event—that biological, biochemical, cultural, sociological, interpersonal, intrapsychic, logical, philosophical, conscious, and unconscious elements are always present—I retain the belief that, in the proper distillation of the event, its essential nature is *psychological*. That is, each suicidal drama occurs in the *mind* of a unique individual. An arboreal image may be useful: See the tree; that tree. There is the chemistry of the soil in which the tree lives. The tree exists in a sociocultural climate. An individual's biochemical states, for example, are its roots, figuratively speaking. An individual's method of committing suicide, the details of the event,

the contents of the suicide note, and so on, are the metaphoric branching limbs, the flawed fruit, and the camouflag-
ing leaves. But the psychological component, the conscious
choice of suicide as the seemingly best solution to a perceived problem, is the main trunk.

The implications of this psychological view are quite ex-
tensive. For one thing, it means that our best route to understanding suicide is not through the study of the structure
of the brain, nor the study of social statistics, nor the study
of mental diseases, but directly through the study of human
emotions described in plain English, in the words of the
suicidal person. The most important question to a potentially
suicidal person is not an inquiry about family history or lab-
oratory tests of blood or spinal fluid, but "Where do you
hurt?" and "How can I help you?"

All of us know that life is sometimes pleasant, usually routine, and too often difficult. This is as true today as it was
in Caesar's time. The positive aspects of life include joy and
happiness, contentment and well-being, success and comfort, good health and creative energy, love and reciprocal
response—life's happy and exhilarating highways and by-
ways.

Much of life is taken up by the routine, pedestrian, everyday, humdrum, habitual, and emotionally neutral stretches
of life—life on automatic pilot, mindlessly cruising along.

And then there is pain and all of life's unhappy aspects:
sorrow, shame, humiliation, fear, dread, defeat, anxiety. The
dark side and dark moments.

When we experience these negative emotions in some
heightened degree, psychological anguish and disturbance
follow. We feel upset, disturbed, perturbed. Everyone has
experienced emotional perturbation at one time or another,
to some degree or another. Unfortunately, some of us live
in a state of constant anguish. Anguish or disturbance or

perturbation is caused by pain, sometimes physical pain, but more often psychological pain. Psychological pain is the basic ingredient of suicide. (But there's a lot more.) Suicide is never born out of exaltation or joy; it is a child of the negative emotions. But in order to begin to understand *suicide*, we need to think about what anguish means, as well as why people entertain thoughts of death, especially death as a way of stopping unbearable misery. Suicidal death, in other words, as an escape from pain. Perturbation and lethality are the bad parents of human self-destruction. Pain is Nature's great signal. Pain warns us; pain both mobilizes us and saps our strength; pain, by its very nature, makes us want to stop it or escape from it.

We can define *lethality* as the likelihood of an individual's being dead by his or her own hand in the near future. *Lethality* is a synonym for *suicidality*: How dangerous is this individual to himself or herself? The purpose of distinguishing these two terms (anguish and lethality) is not only a theoretical one, but a clinical and practical one. When dealing with a highly suicidal person, it is simply not effective to address the lethality directly (through confrontation or exhortation). We can address thoughts about suicide by working with this person and asking why mental turmoil is leading to feelings of lethality. To defuse the situation, to mollify the kindled emotions, is the most effective course. In short, to do anything (within reason) to make that person less perturbed.

Practically every reader of these words has worried about suicide, directly or indirectly; has had moments of concern about a family member, a friend, or oneself. Our constant goal is prevention—but first must come understnding.

A basic rule for us to keep in mind is: We can reduce the lethality if we lessen the anguish, the perturbation. Suicidal individuals who are asked "Where do you hurt?" intuitively know that this is a question about their emotions and their lives, and they answer appropriately, not in biological terms, but with some literary or humanistic sophistication, in psychological terms. What I mean by this is to ask about the person's feelings, worries, and pain.

We can think of these concepts in another way: Perturbation is felt pain; lethality relates to the *idea* of death (nothingness, cessation) as the solution. By itself, mental anguish is not lethal. But lethality, when coupled with elevated perturbation, is a principal ingredient in self-inflicted death. Perturbation supplies the motivation for suicide; lethality is the fatal trigger.

Lethality—the idea that "I can stop this pain; I can kill myself"—is the unique essence of suicide. Anybody who has ever switched off an electric light deliberately to plunge a hideous room into darkness or, with equal deliberation, stopped the action of an annoying engine by turning the key to OFF, has, for that moment, been granted the swift satisfaction the suicidal person hungers for. After all, the suicidal person intends to stop the ongoing activities of *life*.

How is physical pain different from psychological anguish? For one thing, physical pain is not the kind of pain that is centrally involved in suicide. The wish for death by assisted suicide in a person suffering from AIDS or the early stages of Alzheimer's disease is related to the degradations and anxieties attendant to physical pain, rather than to just the physical pain itself, which can be controlled by appropriate doses of medicine.

It is hard to imagine a life without some occasional physical pain. We all know what pain feels like. The scraped knee, the accidental cut or bump, a hard hit on the head. What adults have not cried when they were babies? Many people experience rather intense, severe, even excruciating pain at one time or another, and survive with the memory of it.

Physical pain is a physical or somatic ache or hurt, proceeding from disease or bodily injury or dysfunction—a toothache, earache, stomachache; a cut, fracture, sprain, wound; gout, arthritis, cancer; an "ouch" experience. By pain, we mean physical pain.

There is a vast technical literature on physical pain. One contemporary survey book[1] contains hundreds of references to various kinds of pain: chronic pain, low back pain, phantom limb pain, intractable pain, among other topics. Most large hospitals have special clinics devoted to the management of pain. The control of physical pain is a major concern in the contemporary treatment of human suffering.

Here is an account of pain by a young man dying of AIDS:

> I'm giving up. I want it to be over. I don't expect any miracle anymore. The swelling and the fevers just get me down. . . . And then I'd just like to go to sleep and die. I'm just tired. I woke up this morning. I was really frightened. I was saying, dear God, dear God, what am I going to do? Dear God, dear God, doesn't answer. . . . If there was a way I could end it now, I would do that.

This benighted young man's account of his swelling and fevers is an indirect way of his recounting his physical pain, but it is his fear, his psychological pain that haunts us most. How severe is his physical pain? Many attempts have been made to rate the severity of physical pain. A well-known but simple rating is offered in the McGill-Melzack Pain Questionnaire. In that questionnaire, the basic categories are: no pain, mild, discomforting, distressing, horrible, and excruciating. In effect: mild, moderate, and severe. Such a system tries to help people describe their pain in ordinary words, through the admittedly limited funnel of language, to travel from private inchoate experience to interpersonal communication through the use of culturally defined words and phrases.

Eric Cassell's *The Nature of Suffering and the Goals of Medicine*[2] and David Morris's *The Culture of Pain*[3] are as successful as one can be in capturing the private experience of pain. Cassell—an experienced physician—makes the needed distinction between pain and suffering. The first line of his preface reads: "The test of a system of medicine should be its adequacy in the face of suffering . . . modern medicine fails that test." He argues that the whole person rather than simply the disease should be treated, and persuasively discusses the concept of "personhood." It is a wise and wonderfully written book. Morris—a former professor of literature—gives us an intellectual feast on the meanings, uses, pleasures, and tragedies of pain. It is a mind-stretching experience to read this book, but neither of these first-rate books on pain mentions suicide.

My main purpose in discussing physical pain is to establish that it is *not* the kind of pain that is implicated in most suicide. Which leads us now to the kind of pain that *is* involved—namely, psychological pain, or psychache.

The measurement of psychache—subjective as it is—is admittedly difficult. I have attempted to effect some systematic measure by developing a "Psychological Pain Survey." (See Appendix A.) In creating this form, I have tried to use what psychologists call "The Method of Paired Comparisons" in which an incident (in this case from a Nazi concentration camp) is cited as the anchor point of extreme psychological pain and the person is then asked to rate his or her own psychache in relation to that incident. In this way, we have some objective reference for comparing ratings of different people with one another. To date, I have administered this preliminary form to a number of physicians, clergy, medical students, and undergraduate university students, several hundred in all, without any dire effects on any of them. I have been especially interested in the language—nouns, adjectives, verbs, adverbs—used by individuals who identify themselves at different points along the psychological pain scale, and, of course, most interested in those who identify themselves as suicidal, to whom I have spoken individually.

Let me quote two verbatim accounts of psychological pain. The first is by Beatrice Bessen, a young woman who, as a student in my UCLA undergraduate course on Death and Suicide (which I taught for 20 years), volunteered to complete a Psychological Pain Survey. We had spoken privately and she assured me that she would not be distressed by doing it (and she had her therapist's approval). A photocopy of her Psychological Pain Survey form is reproduced in Appendix A.

At the age of ten I woke up to the horrors of the world. I came out of my childhood innocence and dove head-first into the dark side of life. Recognizing that I was vulnerable to severe pain, and predicting my household was breaking up, I began to pull away from my family. By age 15 I was struggling with self-hate, not understanding what was happening to me. One day my boyfriend abruptly broke up with me. I had never felt such intense pain and I could not handle it. I was alone at home and ran desperately around, panicked over the flood of emotions that was travelling through my body. I ended up taking the kitchen knife into my room and cutting myself, slashes all along my arms. The physical pain let me pull my attention off the emotional agony and I just concentrated on not letting the blood spill over onto the carpet.

The second account is that of a young man written from his hospital bed after he had fortuitously survived a self-inflicted gunshot wound. We'll call him Castro Reyes. He had placed the barrel of a fully automatic pistol near the right side of his head meaning to blow his brains out, but in the tension of the moment he shot erratically and ended up shooting most of his face off. He could not speak, but he could, with effort, write. He was an unusual person: a Caribbean-American, a high school dropout, a scholar about certain aspects of European history, especially ancient Roman history. He was a genuine autodidact, a self-taught master, a young man who wrote polished English and had a command of spelling and grammar and a vocabulary that would have placed him among the top percentiles on most college verbal tests. The hospital staff where I saw him had him incorrectly pegged and treated him (I thought with some disdain) as though he were barely literate. Here, unchanged from his original scrawled text, are some of his penned words:

There was no peace to be found. I had done all I could and was still sinking. I sat many hours seeking answers and all there was was a silent wind and no answers. The answer was clear. Die. I didn't sleep. The dreams were reality and reality dreams. My will to survive and succeed had been crushed and defeated. I was like a general alone on a battlefield being encroached upon by my enemy and its hordes: Fear, hate, self-depreciation, desolation. I felt I had to have the upper hand, to control my destiny, so I sought to die rather than surrender. Destiny and reality began to merge. Those around me were as shadows, bare apparitions, but I was not actually conscious of them, only aware of myself and my plight. Death swallowed me long before I pulled the trigger. I was locked within myself. The world through my eyes seemed to die with me. It was like I was to push the final button to end this world. I committed myself to the arms of Death. There comes a time when all things cease to shine, when the rays of hope are lost. I placed the gun to my head.

What these two people are talking about is psychological pain, or *psychache*. Psychache is the hurt, anguish, or ache that takes hold in the mind. It is intrinsically psychological—the pain of excessively felt shame, guilt, fear, anxiety, loneliness, angst, dread of growing old or of dying badly. When psychache occurs, its introspective reality is undeniable. Suicide happens when the psychache is deemed unbearable and death is actively sought to stop the unceasing flow of painful consciousness. Suicide is a tragic drama in the mind.

What my research has taught me is that only a small minority of cases of excessive psychological pain result in suicide, but every case of suicide stems from excessive psychache.

To understand suicide we must understand suffering and psychological pain and various thresholds for enduring it; to treat suicidal people (and prevent suicide) we must address and then soften and reduce the psychache that drives it. Everyone who commits suicide feels driven to it—indeed, feels that suicide is the *only* option left. All our present well-meaning attention to demographic variables—age, sex, ethnicity, and so on—and all our analysis of the ongoing electrochemical activities of the brain cannot tell us what we centrally want to know about the drama of emotions in the mind, the constricted thinking and the aching for peace. I will focus on the psychological aspects of suicide, where the drama actually unfolds. America's greatest psychologist, William James, said it best (1902): "Individuality is founded in feeling, and the recesses of feeling, the darker, blinder strata of character, are the only places in the world in which we catch real fact in the making, and directly perceive how events occur and how work is actually done"[4]—the "center" of where the "I" lives.

A few years ago, I went back to the Los Angeles County Coroner's Office (where my career as a suicidologist began) to see whether the contents of suicide notes had changed at all in the 40 years since I first studied them. They had not. While it is true, then and now, that many suicide notes do not reflect the anguish associated with the deed and are sometimes pedestrian and even banal, a fair number of suicide notes *do* express the psychological pain that motivates suicide.

Here are a half-dozen suicide notes from men and women; single, married, and separated; ages 24 to 74; death by gunshot, cutting, overdose, and hanging. They reflect the psychological pain of suicide.

Female, 45, married, overdose: "If I haven't the love I want so bad there is nothing left."

Female, 60, single, overdose: "I am tired of this emotional merry-go-round, so I'll get out of it by taking my life."

Female, 74, widowed, cut wrists: "I am powerless over my emotions. Life is unmanageable. I'm like a helpless 12 year old."

Male, 24, married, hanging: "Dear Mary. I am writing these last lines to you because these are the last ones. I really thought that you and little Joe were going to come back into my life but you didn't. I know that you found someone else that is better than me. I hope the son of a bitch dies. I love you very much and Joe too. It hurts a lot that you and I didn't make it. I had a lot of dreams for all of us but they were only dreams. I always thought that dreams would come true but I guess not. I hope to go to heaven but in my case I'll probably go to hell. Please take care of little Joe because I love him with all my heart. Please don't tell him what happened. Tell him I went far away and will come back one of these days. Tell him you don't know when. Well, I guess that's it. Take care of yourself. PS. I know we could have made it but you didn't want to because you wanted to get fucked by someone else well you got it. I can't really say that I hate you or love you. You'll never know. Yours truly, Your husband, George."

Male, 31, separated, hanging: "Forgive me, for today I die. I just cannot live without you. I might as well be dead. Maybe there will be peace. I have this empty feeling inside me that is killing me. I just can't take it anymore. When you left me I died inside. I have to say, nothing left but the broken heart that is leading me into this. I cry to God to help me but he doesn't listen. There is nothing else for me to do."

Male, 49, married gunshot wound to the head: "I sit alone. Now, at last, freedom from the mental torment I have been experiencing. This should come as no surprise. My eyes have spoken for a long, long time of the distress I feel. The rejection, failures and frustrations overwhelm me. There is no way to pull myself out of this hell. Goodbye, love. Forgive me."

In all these notes there is unmistakable psychological pain. Suicide is the result of an interior dialogue. The mind scans its options; the topic of suicide comes up, the mind rejects it, scans again; there is suicide, it is rejected again, and then finally the mind accepts suicide as a solution, then plans it, and fixes it as the only answer. The general word for this process is *introspection*.

Some years ago I was interested in examining the suicidal potential in myself. In the space of three decades I had been hospitalized (for purely physical complaints) in a half-dozen hospitals throughout the United States. I did a rough experiment, using myself as the sole subject. I wanted to know how my psychological needs had changed during hospitalization, and how I had behaved as a patient. Over a period of a few months, in one way or another, I saw my medical folders, concentrating on the nurses' notes that recorded my behavior as a patient.

The results were interesting. In the six hospitals I was viewed in two very distinct ways. In four hospitals I was seen as cooperative, cheerful, even pleasant—reflecting, I believe, the disposition of my psychological needs as I ordinarily move through the world—while in the other two hospitals I was noted as difficult, demanding, uncooperative, irascible— a regular pain in the neck. It became clear to me that the differences devolved not on the quality of care (I was treated well enough in all the hospitals) nor on how sick or close to death I actually was, but on the degree of my fright or terror at the time—my personal, distorted psychological pain.

There was a moment in one hospitalization when one of my physician sons came into the intensive care unit, checked my flagging vital signs, and obtained emergency medical help that saved my life, when I did not sense any danger (or was too sedated to recognize it) and was, at least from the nurses' point of view, a pussycat.

In my two exceptionally stormy hospitalizations there was a radical shift among my psychological needs (from my usual needs for achievement, nurturance, play, order, etc.) to a sudden heightening of my needs for control, inviolacy, and understanding. ("What the hell is going on around here?") In other words, when I was frightened, there was a shift to my omega needs that I would fight for and be willing to get ugly about; my backed-in-the-corner personality of holler and bluster. That was the Mr. Hyde side of me—my re-orientation of my psychological needs in time of perceived threat and felt stress. It was my fight-or-flight personality that I rarely show to the world.

This little study gave me some valuable insights into the theoretical scenario of what needs I could become suicidal about. Further, it showed me personally how an individual can shift into a special (life-threatening) mode of reasoning if those alarms are connected (as they were not in my case) with the *idea* of death as the desired surcease. I saw again that suicide is a drama in the introspecting mind.

William James wrote persuasively, in 1890, about "the stream of consciousness."[5] In contemporary terms, we might refer to it as the TV set that runs throughout all our waking (and dreaming) moments. That is what "being awake" op-erationally means; it means that you are introspecting. An especially good definition of introspection is from Aldous Huxley's novel *Eyeless in Gaza* (1936): "Those images on the other side of the eyes that go on living that private life of theirs, undisturbed."[6] After all, suicide is the desire to reduce painful tension by stopping the unbearable flow of consciousness.

The eminent Canadian psychologist, Donald O. Hebb, wrote that the mind is what the brain does.[7] That is very good, but it is too limiting. The mind is what the brain does—and more. The mind has a mind of its own. The main business of the mind is to mind its own business. Mind—unlike kidney, skin, or lungs and unlike urine, sweat, or car-bon dioxide—is not another kind of "stuff." Mind is the process (called thoughts and feelings) that takes place in liv-ing brain cells. As the skin produces sweat, the liver bile, and the pancreas insulin, so, in a roughly comparable, almost metaphoric way, the brain—that marvelous organ of billions of cells—"secretes" consciousness. Except that unlike bile or insulin, thoughts and feelings are not things. They are pure process. Descartes confused the issue by talking about *res extenso* (extended things) and *res mentis* (mental things); there *are* no mental *things*.

Obviously, no brain, no mind. But slicing Jeffrey Dahmer's brain will no more explain the mysteries of his gross psychological pathology than slicing Einstein's brain will yield $E=mc^2$. On the other hand, severe depression, melancholia, psychoses, and bipolar depressions are related to disorders of brain physiology or even brain structure, but *suicide* is an essentially mental process in the mind—a topic of interest to all health professionals and many thousands of ordinary people, people who are otherwise quite healthy.

Suicide rests largely on psychological pain. And the primary source of severe psychache is frustrated psychological needs. Obviously, a critical segment of our behavior is based on our fundamental biological needs—for oxygen, for food, for water, and for a livable temperature. But once these are met, our actions are motivated by our need to reduce inner tensions by satisfying an array of psychological needs. These include the intangible needs to achieve, to affiliate, to dominate, to avoid harm, to be autonomous, to be loved and succored, to understand what is going on—among others. We live our lives in pursuit of psychological needs. When an individual commits suicide, that person is trying to blot out psychological pain that stems from thwarted psychological needs "vital" for that person.

Henry A. Murray, in *Explorations in Personality* (1938)—one of the most important books in American psychology—first formulated these psychological needs that we spend our lifetimes pursuing. Murray asked, "For what is suicide but an action to put an end to intolerable emotions?" In his book, Murray leisurely presents, defines, discusses, and illustrates a score of these dynamic elements of personality. He defines a *need* as "a force in the brain which organizes perception and intellection in such a way as to appease or satisfy the organism."[8]

All our activities at home, in school, on the streets, on the job, during the day, after hours, and in our dreams and fantasies, are expressions of these needs that, to one degree or another, motivate our lives. Suicide is always an aspect of a larger life pattern.

Each of us has an idiosyncratic disposition made up of psychological needs. Indeed, we can say that the relative weights we give these psychological needs is a window into our personality. It reflects what makes us tick.

Admittedly, it does some violence to the complexities of Murray's rich text to reduce hundreds of pages of his elegant prose to a list on a single sheet, but I have done so in the interests of accessibility and practical clinical application. (See the Psychological Need Form that is briefly presented in Table 1 and more fully explicated in Appendix B.) I have created a simple form on which I have listed these needs so that I could rate my subjects and patients to indicate how these various needs influenced their view of themselves and their world.

To set some parameters, I used this form to rate each person by assigning numbers (weights) to the 20 needs so that the numbers added up to exactly 100. In other words, everyone gets the same score. It is the differences among the needs (within that individual) that yield the interesting information and show us how needs shape the pattern of our lives. Essentially, this simple form provides a means for us to think about what is really important to us and those we wish to understand.

Obviously, with this form you can rate a wide variety of people. You can rate yourself, your patient, your loved one,

Table 1   Murray Need Form

Subject _____ Sex ___ Age ___ Rater _____ Date _____

_____ ABASEMENT   The need to submit passively; to belittle self.

_____ ACHIEVEMENT   To accomplish something difficult; to overcome.

_____ AFFILIATION   To adhere to a friend or group; to affiliate.

_____ AGGRESSION   To overcome opposition forcefully; fight, attack.

_____ AUTONOMY   To be independent and free; to shake off restraint.

_____ COUNTERACTION   To make up for loss by restriving; get even.

_____ DEFENDANCE   To vindicate the self against criticism or blame.

_____ DEFERENCE   To admire and support, praise, emulate a superior.

_____ DOMINANCE   To control, influence, and direct others; dominate.

_____ EXHIBITION   To excite, fascinate, amuse, entertain others.

_____ HARMAVOIDANCE   To avoid pain, injury, illness, and death.

_____ INVIOLACY   To protect the self and one's psychological space.

_____ NURTURANCE   To feed, help, console, protect, nurture another.

_____ ORDER   To achieve organization and order among things and ideas.

_____ PLAY   To act for fun; to seek pleasure for its own sake.

_____ REJECTION   To exclude, banish, jilt, or expel another person.

_____ SENTIENCE   To seek sensuous, creature-comfort experiences.

_____ SHAME-AVOIDANCE   To avoid humiliation and embarrassment.

_____ SUCCORANCE   To have one's needs gratified; to be loved.

_____ UNDERSTANDING   To know answers; to know the hows and whys.

100

Source: Adapted from Henry A. Murray, *Explorations in Personality* (New York: Oxford University Press, 1938).

a friend, a current public figure, a historical figure, a fictional character—anyone. You can rate a person when he or she is functioning fairly well or when that person is acutely suicidal. (As we will see, the therapy for a suicidal person is tailor-made to address the frustrated needs that fuel the psychological pain, which in turn drives suicidal thoughts.)

I have attempted to illustrate how this works by looking at the disposition or weights of these needs within some well-known personalities. (See Table 2.) What gives these ratings special force is the professional who is rating each historic figure. Here is the list of professionals along with the individuals I asked them to rate using the Murray Need Form.

- Napoleon, rated by Eugen Weber, Professor of History at UCLA, an authority on French civilization.

- Hitler, rated by Frederick Redlich, psychiatrist, former Dean of the Yale School of Medicine, who is writing a medical biography of Hitler.

- Freud, rated by Robert R. Holt, Freud scholar; Professor of Psychology Emeritus, New York University.

- Marilyn Monroe, rated by Robert E. Litman, psychiatrist-psychoanalyst, who conducted the psychological autopsy of Monroe's death; former President of the American Association of Suicidology.

- Captain Ahab (the chief protagonist of *Moby-Dick*), rated by Alfred Kazin, author and one of America's foremost literary critics.

- Herman Melville, rated by Hershel Parker, Melville scholar, who is writing a definitive biography of Melville.

Table 2   Ratings of Psychological Needs
of a Dozen Eminent Individuals

	Napoleon Bonaparte	Adolph Hitler	Sigmund Freud	Marilyn Monroe	Capt. Ahab
Abasement		1	0	7	
Achievement	20	10	11	8	20
Affiliation		2	5	2	
Aggression	10	10	6	2	10
Autonomy	10	7	8	5	10
Counteraction	10	10	7	2	10
Defendance	2	5	8	3	10
Deference		1	2	10	
Dominance	20	7	10	2	10
Exhibition	5	6	6	16	10
Harmavoidance		2	2	2	
Inviolacy		6	3	4	
Nurturance		1	4	2	
Order	11	3	4	2	
Play		3	2	6	
Rejection		7	4	2	10
Sentience	2	5	1	2	
Shame-avoidance		5	5	3	
Succorance		4	3	12	
Understanding	10	5	9	2	10

Note: Each column totals 100 points.

- Lyndon Baines Johnson, rated by Irving Bernstein, Professor Emeritus of Political Science at UCLA, who has written a history of the Johnson presidency.
- Jane Addams, rated by Harry Wasserman, Professor Emeritus of Social Welfare at UCLA.

Herman Melville	Lyndon Johnson	Jane Addams	Jim Jones	Martha Graham	Vincent Van Gogh	Richard Feynman
7	1	1	1	1	9	1
10	16	12	4	10	11	15
3	3	12	1	6	4	2
6	5	3	12	3	7	1
11	5	7	8	10	7	10
3	4	1	4	1	7	1
3	5	1	12	3	4	2
3	2	5	1	1	5	1
2	12	5	12	10	2	4
4	6	3	11	6	6	10
3	5	5	2	1	1	2
11	5	5	4	10	5	3
3	2	5	1	3	9	2
2	3	9	2	10	5	5
3	2	7	1	2	1	10
2	4	2	6	3	2	1
8	7	2	5	3	1	5
4	3	3	9	2	2	3
2	8	5	3	5	10	2
10	2	9	1	10	2	20

- Jim Jones, rated by Louis Jolyon West, Professor of Psychiatry at UCLA and an expert on cults.
- Martha Graham, rated by Alma Hawkins, Professor and Chair Emerita, Department of Dance, UCLA.
- Vincent Van Gogh, rated by William McKinley Runyan, Professor in the School of Social Welfare

at the University of California at Berkeley and an expert on the topic of biography.

- Richard Feynman, rated by David Saxon, Professor Emeritus of Physics at UCLA, and former President of the University of California.

Most of the ratings represent how the person functioned, more or less successfully, over a period of time in adulthood. There are, of course, some suicides in this list: Hitler, Monroe, Jones, Van Gogh, and Napoleon, who attempted suicide (by poison) after Waterloo. This leads us to the observation that among these psychological needs we can distinguish two kinds: first, those weighted needs that characterize the functioning, ongoing personality; the needs the person *lives with*, the *modal* needs. Second, there are those needs the individual focuses on when he or she is under duress, suffering heightened inner tension and in mental pain. These are the needs an individual is willing to *die for*, the *vital* needs. When a person becomes suicidal, the inner focus shifts from one's ordinary (modal) needs to frustrated or thwarted needs that arise, in that person, with the perception of threat, failure, duress, pain, emergency—the psychological needs deemed by that individual as vital for continued living. Each one of us is capable of filling out the form to represent our ordinary needs and our "emergency" disposition of needs, whose frustration might lead us to suicide.

With 20 needs, one might think that there might be 20 "kinds" of suicide. In practice, as few as 10 or 12 of these needs are implicated in suicide. Murray's concepts (and the Psychological Need Form) provide a way of identifying which needs are central in any particular case and allow us to enter the mind of the person by focusing on those needs. We can begin to identify instances of suicide in terms of the main frustrated needs that are involved.

For practical purposes, most suicides tend to fall into one of five clusters of psychological needs. They reflect different kinds of psychological pain.

- Thwarted *love*, acceptance, and belonging—related to frustrated needs for succorance and affiliation.

- Fractured *control*, predictability, and arrangement— related to frustrated needs for achievement, autonomy, order, and understanding.

- Assaulted self-image and the avoidance of *shame*, defeat, humiliation, and disgrace—related to frustrated needs for affiliation, defendance, and shame-avoidance.

- Ruptured key relationships and the attendant *grief* and bereftness—related to frustrated needs for affiliation and nurturance.

- Excessive *anger*, rage, and hostility—related to frustrated needs for dominance, aggression, and counteraction.

But there are more than five kinds of suicide and each sad case should be assessed and understood in terms of its own idiosyncratic details.

The ratings by the professionals of the historical figures merit our close study. Readers may find it intellectually interesting to peruse the weightings of psychological needs for some favorite heroes or despised villains, and to agree or disagree with those given by an expert—and then to ponder what ratings would apply to the reader's own "ordinary" self and his or her theoretical "suicidal" self, if life turned sour and self-destruction seriously came to mind.

In the following chapters, we consider, in some detail, the disposition of psychological needs for three special people, Ariel Wilson, Beatrice Bessen, and Castro Reyes—of course, these are not their real names—who are the three main "case presentations" of this book. It all comes together, with general implications for possible rescue, in Chapter 8. We turn now to a discussion of Ariel Wilson, a young woman who set herself on fire.

2

The Need to be Loved: The Case of Ariel Wilson

How do we begin to understand the needs and psychological pain that drive a person to suicide? The case study has a long-honored tradition in psychology, and so we look in detail at the case of Ariel Wilson, a young woman who attempted to take her life by setting herself on fire.

Her own life and death are dramatic almost beyond measure, but the interaction between us was not without its own drama. Some years ago I had given a workshop on suicide prevention in a rather remote place in one of the mountain states. At the noon break a young woman came up and asked to talk to me, privately. Ariel's appearance was somewhat unusual, certainly memorable. She had a lovely face, touched with brooding—she reminded me of a young Dolores Del Rio, the movie actress of my youth—pale skin and ebony hair. She wore a floor-length dress, blue, with tiny white polka-dots; the sleeves were to her wrists, trimmed with lace; at her throat, a choker collar, decorated with the same white lace. At one moment, when we were seated in a quiet place, talking, she undid her collar and her sleeves and from what I saw I could estimate that, except for her lovely hands and face, every part of her was covered with angry keloid scars. When I asked, "What happened?" she answered simply, "I immolated myself."

I arranged to send her a tape recorder and some tapes for her to tell her story, as she wished to do. Months went by; no word. I decided to telephone her, but there was no answer no matter what hour I called over a period of a few days. I became uneasy, and finally telephoned the chief of police in her small town to get her telephone number. To my complete astonishment, he told me that she had died a few days before. Gone! And then, incredulously, a week later, posted by an anonymous sender, the cassette machine and six completed tapes arrived in the mail, as a posthumous gift. I listened to them with tears. And when I collected my thoughts, I came to see Ariel as a woman whose central need was succorance—a need so intense that it caused her to take her own life.

What is *succorance*? Simply put, it is the need to be taken care of, to be loved and succored. It is the theme that is woven all through Ariel Wilson's life—her hunger for it; her inability to obtain it; her frustration with her unfulfilled need for it; her willingness to die for it; and her fiery resolution of this unrequited need.

The need for succorance can be defined as the desire "to have one's needs gratified by the sympathetic aid of another;

to be supported, sustained, guided, consoled, taken care of; comforted, protected."[1] In short, to be loved.

A definitive discussion of succorance can be found in the work of Henry A. Murray. The text is in a rather arcane source, Murray's unpublished biography of *his* obsession, Herman Melville, written in the 1920s. The original pages are in the Murray Archives at Harvard; a copy was lent to me by Forrest Robinson, the author of the recent biography of Murray.[2] Here is Murray's definition of succorance:

> The *need for succorance* [grows from] the desire for a congenial, trustworthy, nourishing, loving supporter. The function of the supporter (who is activated by the *need for nurturance*) is to administer to the subject's other needs: for food, money, affection, harmavoidance, and so forth. . . . The need is accompanied by feelings of helplessness, of impotence, of forlornness, of forsakenness, of distress, and by the "anxiety of insupport." The typical objectifications of the drive are these: weeping, cries for help, clinging, bids for sympathy, exhibitions of pain and misery, pleadings for assistance, mercy and generosity. Succorance is related to the need for passivity; it leads to a dependent attitude. In many cases the succorance drive is subsidiary to the *need for affiliation* (a basic tendency, whose aim is to establish and maintain friendly relationships with others). . . . The succorance need is completely satisfied in the womb (as is the need for passivity), and nearly so when the child is dependently sucking nourishment from the mother's breast. The activity of the drive is essential to the infant's welfare; to call the mother when hungry, hurt, sick, cold, damp. Premonitions of frustrations lead the child to depend on the mother's presence and feel anxious, homesick or forlorn when she is absent.
>
> The most primitive kind of support is physical: solid ground (*terra firma*), a wide and even path, a railing; something substantial to touch, stand on, grasp, rest against or be

enveloped by. Hence the most elementary form of the need for succorance is physical, being accompanied by the fear of "voids": open spaces below or around. Loss of support and falling is a universal stimulus for extreme fear in a child. But since in the first months physical support is largely furnished by the mother—her womb, her enclosing arms, her nipple, her hand when learning to walk, her skirts and "apron strings"—the need for succorance in its human form predominates.

We might ask whether all psychological needs are created equal. Probably not. Some needs seem to be more preeminent than others. I am thinking of the needs for affection, respect, appreciation, admiration, and attention, especially when they are coupled with the psychological needs for sanctuary, safety, and freedom from fear and anxiety.

It was not the mere presence of the need for succorance in Ariel Wilson that mattered so; it was the prominence, the intensity, and the singular importance of this particular need that shaped her personality and influenced her life course.

Here, in her own words, we hear her story. With all her sense of sophistication, we can detect her small-town upbringing and self-defeating traits of character. What follows is a verbatim report (with slight editing and added section headings) of the audiotapes that arrived after she was dead. We will listen to this troubled memoir with our "third ear," attuned to her faulty thinking and trying to enter into her private world so that we might understand why suicide became the only course of action she could take.

General Background and Previous Suicidal Behavior

My name is Ariel Wilson. These tapes are about an incident of my trying to immolate myself. I'll try to make it as explicit as possible of what I remember occurred that evening. For some months, from probably August up to December. I really didn't feel any happiness or any good feelings about myself. I believe in October I had attempted suicide. I took an overdose of NoDoz and aspirin, and I thought I would have heart failure, which I didn't. I remember being very upset.

My roommate and I were living together and I left this note saying, Don't look for me. Come in the bedroom later on and there will be a surprise for you. And she came into the bedroom, and of course I wasn't dead, I was just very ill. She had actually made an appointment for me to see a mental health worker but I made some silly excuse of why I couldn't go and I never did go.

That takes me up to December and things weren't going very well for me: Job, social life, personal life, and there were some precipitating factors. Early in December I had dinner with a man who wanted to be engaged to me but I had declined his engagement ring. And I had a dinner date with him. He had come 100 miles to see me. He was still in love with me in many ways. I wasn't in love with him and it was a somewhat nice evening but in some ways it was kind of unhappy for me. And this was early December and I had told him that I could not go home at Christmas time, which was making me terribly unhappy. He was making arrangements so that I could go home with him for Christmas and he was very delighted that I would be with him for the holidays.

However, I was not very happy about it. I had made the arrangements but it was just not something that I wanted to do. I had discussed with my mother that I wanted to go home very badly and I was hurting very badly but she kept telling me that it would cost too much money, 30 dollars for the bus ticket, that it was not worth it because I would be coming home to go to school in February anyway, and I could wait until then and that it wasn't necessary to make this extra trip home. And

I couldn't explain to her that I really didn't want to go home to go to school there, for one thing; and second of all, I just wanted to be at home at Christmas time in a protected environment, and I was very upset that I had to make other arrangements.

Death of Father

Another facet of the burning I think that should be mentioned is that my father died. He was accidentally shot in the chest when I was 16 and I found him and it was December just before Christmas. It was almost identically the same day that I tried to immolate myself three years later. Whether or not there is any correlation between that I don't know. I know I dwelled on the fact before I attempted suicide that it sort of was the right season. It was the time of year when the hurts come out and I had some bad feelings for my father and it just seemed like it all fit together. He died then and I would die then.

I have to discuss more the way my father died and how I was involved in it. After the immolation I saw a psychiatrist and it all came out that I really did love my father. I thought I hated him. I was very upset with him, but he was dead, and it came out that I really do think I loved him. I wasn't mature enough to accept the fact that he couldn't accept love from a child. And he was having problems himself. It was a very poor relationship and it was dissolved before I understood these things.

I'd like to talk a little bit about how my father died. In some ways it's quite important and also I have resolved it in some ways. I was 16 and going to high school. So one morning I got up, dressed and I just had this enormous feeling that my father was dead. Now, whether I wished him dead I don't know, but I just had this feeling, very uncomfortable and very nervous inside. So I walked through the house except for his bedroom.

My mother and father slept in separate bedrooms. My father came and went as he pleased. He would be gone for maybe two or three days at a time and we wouldn't know where he'd be and it wasn't unusual that he would be gone. We would never ask him where he would go because we would always get a snide remark that it was none of our business and to let him be. So we had learned not to ask him. And so I don't know why, it was just odd to me that he hadn't been home. And I woke my mother up and I told her that I thought something was really wrong. I thought my father was dead and that he was in his room. And she said, Oh don't be silly, I'll go in there with you. And so she did. There he was, frozen still in a pool of blood.

My mother went immediately into the kitchen and started calling people. She wasn't sure of really what happened. And what did happen was that he was cleaning an old revolver at his desk, and it was a faulty gun, it was a really old gun, and not well kept up. And it had fallen over on the seat and fallen on a little tab or something on the seat and shot him in the chest as he was trying to catch it.

He died instantly, from what we understood from the coroner's report, and it was proved that it was not suicide. However, he had threatened suicide and he had talked about it with my aunt, his sister, and with my mother, and we were all quite aware of it, so my mother was quite sure he had committed suicide. Well, my aunt, who lives very close, she came down and was with us and she stood and told me that I had killed my father, and he had committed suicide because of me.

My father and I had been in a row earlier in the fall, but my aunt really stunned me by saying that I had killed my father. So it was something that was put on me. Now, whether I believed it or not, that I had played a part in it, I really don't know, but I know that I was greatly hurt by it. It was just hard for me to take. It was so violent and it was so quick and it was so hard to accept. It was just kind of unreal.

The row that we had been into earlier in the fall was that my father was saying that I was breaking him, I was costing him way too much money and that he couldn't afford to keep me. I was very upset by it and I had made arrangements that I would go away and I would live in a foster home and I would work and go to high school. But my mother wouldn't allow me to. She said I had to stay at home where I belonged, that I couldn't leave in spite of whatever. But my father had been trying to push me out for quite some time and I had supported myself quite well for clothes and school supplies and different articles that I had earned through baby sitting, through waitressing, but he and I just weren't getting along at that time. We were having some difficulties and I know that he wasn't communicating in any way. So there it left me with my father dead.

Also, the other factor that was existing at that time was that my father was calling me a whore, that I was, you know, a loose woman because I was dating and that I was screwing around. And the fact was that I had actually gone with only a few guys at the time I was 16, and I had slept with no one. And I think after he died, my way of getting back was that he died in December and on January first I made sure I lost my virginity.

Mother

My mother is a very dominant person. Yet she'll say always that she really didn't want to be that strong, but I think that's a bunch of bullshit. She's always been domineering. She's always been aggressive and she really didn't allow my father to stand up. However, I think he had his problems too and he really couldn't. So I don't know. It's six of one and half-a-dozen of the other. As I see it honestly, as I evaluate it myself—like I've asked my uncle who knew my father way back when, and he said he was a very nice man—I wish I could have known that niceness, because I think I missed out. My mother kind of turned him into being hateful in a way. She pushed him that way, and he was kind of sad.

And there was always just a conflict, and this conflict was money. My mother was very manipulating with money. She uses money as a weapon, but my father, he was just very miserly. He thought it was a big deal if once a month he threw you a dollar. He would just literally throw it at you. It was just a big smart-alecky thing, like he was doing you such a favor. But he was such a kid himself that it was just sad. He worked so damned hard and his life was really unfulfilled, very unhappy in many ways. My mother has never really accepted his death, I don't think. I mean he is dead in all ways, but she hated him and she despised him and she was going to leave him and she fought with him. But in his death he holds her. Had she left him before, she could have left with a clean slate, but as it was he died on her suddenly and so now she hangs on for her dear life to many of the memories of things that he liked and things he hung on to. A prime example of that is that she isolates herself and works like a knothead. I feel it's kind of unhealthy for her to be so isolated all the time and working so hard at her age. It's not right, but that's the way she is.

Row with Father

My mother took good care of him physically. She always had meals for him, she always had clothes for him, but she was so mean to him in lots of ways. Like one time my father and I had gotten into a row. That was earlier in the year that I was 16, and I had wanted a car and I had chosen one and I had decided that I needed one and I was a bit spoiled, I guess, and wanted my own way. And he and I were talking about it and he sort of turned, his eyes just got black, and he just got into this rage and he just hollered at me, You're just like your mother, and he was saying such ugly things about me. His eyes were so black I was really frightened. I just thought he was going to kill me. And he hit me across the face. I tried to get out of the car he was driving and I couldn't, he held me in.

And all of a sudden after he hit me he calmed down just like that. It was just like a peace came over him. He released his anger or something and he was apologizing over and over again and by this time I was becoming quite hysterical and crying and just mad, madder than hell that how dare he strike me, and he kept pleading with me not to tell my mother, and of course I did. I went home immediately and told her and she kept him up until three or four in the morning hollering at him, how stupid to do that to the child over nothing. She would carry on things from way far past, things that had happened years ago, and held a grudge. This is how she dealt with him and she was just an unbelievable fighter. It was just an ugly fight. And yet if he defended himself, which many times he did, he was just as nasty too, and he would call her all dirty different names too. So the situation was kind of sad. And I have to admit that after he was dead, after a period of time my feelings about it were that I was sort of happy for him in a way, that his misery was gone.

Cemeteries and Death

A few years back my mother and I went out in the country and I have this thing about cemeteries, I guess. I really like old cemeteries and this relates mostly to my father and it was kind of putting things together for me. It's an incident that was really important to me. We were in this old cemetery, and what was interesting and unique about this cemetery is that it is very old and the crosses are wooden and they were rotting away and they were waving in the breeze and they were just—just gorgeous really, just really fine, classical gravemarkers and the daisies were blooming and the grasses were growing tall on the graves and the breeze was blowing and I was just so impressed by the earthiness of it and life, of this part of death. And I thought it was nifty but then I looked over aways to the newer part of the cemetery where the grass was clipped. It was kept well and it was clipped short and it looked so stilted, so guilty. And I was thinking that in one of these older graves finally there is no man to control it all. It seems like in life man tries to control when death occurs also. Even though we can't control our own death, we try to control our feelings about other people's deaths. And when God or whoever, in quotes—Nature, let's say Mother Nature—was able to take over, she said it so much better, she was able to do it gracefully and graciously and time it in this circle that life and death, this body in the earth created new life and it was put together, it was a completed circle. Whereas when you see the clipped grass, it's almost sad, it's almost a guilt feeling. It's almost like people have to hang on. They have to control because it's their way of saying that they still care and I thought, Wow, you know, they don't allow those people to die. They don't allow those people to complete the circle of life and death, and I think I put it together for my father, and that he went back to the soil and it was O.K. And at last I felt good about it, that it was O.K., it was something I could never change and it's something that I don't ever want to change and I don't regret it. It's something that happened and I accept it now.

The Day of the Incident

I guess that brings me up to the date of the incident. I remember being very unhappy that week. Things were not working out. I was not working. I recall it was very cold. I was without money. Friends were not helping me a whole lot. I was not getting along well with them. However, I really wasn't fighting with them. But I had various friends that I did know and it just seemed like they just really didn't have time for me and I was hurting very badly inside and it just was an overwhelming desire, I guess, to die.

And I know that I debated about this death around two or three months. I had planned and planned and planned and of course the attempt earlier in October did not work out, so it just added to it. It frustrated me even further that I wasn't able to die. So what was going through my mind was that I would burn myself.

I had read somewhere in the newspapers that the people in Vietnam committed suicide by burning themselves. It was just a sure deal that they would die. And I think it went through my mind that this was how I was going to do it. And part of the reason was that I knew it was a sure deal. There was no way of surviving. So this is why I made the decision and I sort of dwelled on it. It was just something that I thought and thought about a lot, and I really hadn't picked a day at all. It was just something that I was kind of waiting out.

The Day

On that day I don't recall getting up early in the morning. By this time I had gotten most of my things together, my books, my clothing, the things that I owned, my personal possessions, the little odds and ends, knicknacks that I had collected, some paintings and different ceramic items, things that were meaningful to me. And everything was very well organized and I remember, later on in the afternoon, everything was well put together. I remember being semitearful and just down in the mouth but I had energy. I had energy that I could do things. I was able to function.

It was probably toward evening when this all came about. I had been quite upset, but I wasn't crying. I wasn't taking any action, but I just really wasn't feeling very well. I was just feeling very bad and sad for myself and very sorry for myself. Things were just not happening. Things were not working out.

Her Ex-Boyfriend

Then, at six o'clock, this woman, Mrs. Brown, called me. She had been drinking some. Mrs. Brown, in relation to me, was the mother of an ex-boyfriend of mine, but actually at the time I considered him a boyfriend and somebody that I thought I cared a whole lot about and worried a whole lot about and wanted him to love me so badly, but he didn't. He was 26 years old at the time. I was 19. He was going to school full time at the time, along with working a full-time job. And he had more or less played me for laughs, had used me, had taken advantage of me sexually and otherwise. I thought I had been good to him and I had given him all, all my feelings, all my hopes, all my desires, all my dreams, and yet he sort of laughed at it. He sort of took advantage of it and walked away, like, Well, that's how it is, sweetie, that's how life is. Some people are takers and some people are givers, and you're a giver and I'm a taker. At that time I really didn't know how to cope with it. I was very, very upset and was almost bitter in some ways, but I wanted him so badly. By this time in December I was well aware that he had been dating other girls but that still didn't impress upon me that he no longer had any cares for me.

The Final Straw

So this particular evening his mother had called me and she was going on and on about a Christmas present that a girlfriend had given him. It was a gold watch that he was so impressed with and felt it was the most beautiful gift that he could ever receive. And what was going through my mind at that time was that I feel that I am a very generous person and I would give almost anybody anything that would make them very happy and I would give them almost anything feeling-wise, anything of myself. And I had wanted to give him a lovely, lovely Christmas present and in the back of my mind I had set my goals for it to be a stereo that I wanted to give him. But of course I had no money, or very little money, just mere sustenance, that's about all. I didn't have anything. That I really couldn't consider giving him a stereo in any way and that was really breaking my heart.

But I really could not give him anything that was really very meaningful because of lack of money. So I had bought him a record called "Good Night Sweetheart," which was meaningful to me in a way, but it was a very sad record but this was all I could offer him. And I knew at the time that it would not have been impressive to him at all. And Mrs. Brown was going on about this watch and how great it was and how her son felt so much and thought so much of this girl.

And I started sobbing on the phone. I was sobbing for myself and feeling that I really was a nothing. I really had nothing to offer. I could in no way compete. I could in no way share a love with this guy and I was just very broken-hearted and I was very upset and I started to sob.

And she finally sensed that I was very upset and I couldn't

tell her and she went on and on and asked me what was wrong. And she said, Well, why don't you come over and maybe you'll feel better, come over, I don't want you crying, and I said, Oh, no, I'll be all right, and I sort of contained myself. So finally we terminated the conversation.

Almost immediately, she had her husband call me. And he called me by a pet name he had for me and he was kind of cute little man in a way, and he pleaded with me to come over because he knew I was upset. And to pacify him I said certainly, I would be over in 15 minutes.

It was like the straw that broke the camel's back. I sort of had had enough piled on me that I really couldn't handle it. That was all I could take. It was just enough. There was no more that I wanted to hear. There was no more that I wanted to see. There was no more that I wanted to live and I knew that the only out was death. And at this time I made the decision, that evening about six o'clock.

I had no interruptions. There was nobody to hold me back in any way, that would change my mind, that this is what I had to do. I put on a nylon bathrobe, and the thought that was going through my mind was that I couldn't possibly ruin my clothes because that would be very selfish. Somebody certainly could use them other than myself, even though I knew I wouldn't be around. But I couldn't ruin any items that would be useful to other people. So I put on a very thin nylon bathrobe and I did have a brassiere on and underpants and I did put on an old pair of loafers. It was very cold outside and I did put on a coat.

Her Friends

I had an electric toaster that I had to return to some friends' house which was a few blocks away. So I got into the car and at the time I took a glass gallon jug, and took it with me along with the toaster. I remember kind of shaking when I was getting the jug because I think I was a bit afraid. I was a bit nervous that I had made the decision. I was kind of scared, almost like I had to do it. It was something I was forced into in a way and yet it was something I knew I had to accomplish.

So I took the toaster to these friends' house and they were home. I remember just walking in and walking through the house and by this time I was sobbing again. And not one word was said to me by these people. I think there were around four people in the house. And I just walked through the house, put the toaster on the kitchen table and walked right out. And nobody touched my arm, nobody asked what's wrong, nobody even gestured, and it upset me even more that this was sort of the end. Nobody really reached out for me in any way, and I think at that time I really must have been reaching out, I must have been saying, You know I am really upset. I am really having problems. Help me. But at that time nobody responded.

I remember getting back in the car and feeling ever so much alone because these were my friends and even they did not care, even they did not want to share my sadness, and even they wanted no part of me. When I was happy, it was fine, but if I was sad it did not make any difference and they didn't realize the extent of my thoughts or my feelings.

I then drove to a gas station and bought a gallon of gas. And no questions were asked. And I took the gallon of gas in my car and drove back to my apartment building and I parked my car.

The Event Itself

It seemed like I moved slowly at that time. It wasn't real quick movement, physical movement, it seemed like I was moving in slow motion almost. I was making these decisions and I don't remember thinking of my sadness or the things that were breaking my heart. It was kind of like the end of things I was thinking about, that I would be no more, that I would hurt no more. It was going to be good. It was going to be something that would fulfill me. I was going to be strong and be able to perform something. A lot of things were going through my head but I remember not sobbing at this time. I was not upset any longer in that way. I was not releasing it by tears.

I remember sitting in the car for just a second and it was sort of like a blank in my mind. I don't remember thinking about a whole lot of things, but I felt very calm. I felt very good. I felt a kind of hush over my body, that it was going to be O.K.

And then I remember pouring the gasoline first over the front seat and then over the back seat and just sprinkling it and of course over myself to a great extent, and I laid the jar then on the seat. Then I got the matches out, and even then no thoughts went through my head at all of the pain that it was going to entail, the misery, the hurt, any of that. It amazes me now that I really didn't think that burns would really hurt, but none of that went through my head. It just felt good. It was the first time, in fact, that I felt at peace, that I wasn't hurting inside. At times before that it felt like I had just been stabbed and was bleeding and people were just watching me bleed, seeing the blood flow, and almost laughing, saying, ha, ha, that's your problem. And for once it seemed like I had taken care of my problems and no one had to watch my sores anymore and that my pain would just go away. It was not going to exist anymore, especially my mental pain.

I opened the match box and struck one match and it would not light. It was soaked with gas and I sort of smiled to myself thinking, Well, I'll have to try a second one. And I remember very slowly striking the second one and it did strike and it did light. And at that instant the fumes ignited, just a tremendous explosion. It was an overwhelming sound. The sound was terribly loud. It was almost a gush. It was like a very heavy pressure being pressed against my body and then immediately I felt the pain. I felt a sudden surge of just cringing, and as I look at my burn scars now I must have flexed my whole body in an almost protective position. But the pain was unbelievable. It was just over my whole body. It was just such a sudden pressure of heat and flame and it just really hurt and the noise was so loud.

I remember holding my breath because I couldn't stand the smell of the gasoline. So I did hold my breath, which I understand did help in saving me because had my lungs been burned, I would have been dead. But I did hold my breath because I could not stand the smell of the gasoline and I did stand the surge of heat. Well, by the second surge—it surged once and I don't know how many seconds that entailed, but the second surge—oh, God, oh God, the pain by this time was just so magnanimous [sic] I just couldn't stand it any longer and I was almost reaching for the door to push myself out, because at that moment it wasn't very peaceful and it was hurting so badly, but I don't recall crying out. I don't think I screamed. I don't think I hollered. It was silent except for this ignition of the car. It was just so loud.

Aftermath

There were two or three people who were across the street and they saw the car ignite and they came rushing over, I believe; I didn't see them. But they came rushing over and they opened the door very fast. That was the second surge of heat and they pulled me out and rolled me on the ground as fast as they could. And they were, I remember them, shouting and were very excited. And by this time they were rolling me on the ground and it was cold and damp and it was wintery, and I didn't have much clothes on by this time.

And I remember looking down at myself and I was just shocked. I saw this skin, just layers of skin, hanging off my arms and off my chest. It just seemed like huge triangles, like pie crusts, just hanging off of me, of this singed, curled skin, and it was almost yellowish. These people were immediately saying, What a horrible accident, what a horrible accident, and I'm hollering saying, But it wasn't. I wanted to die. I wanted to die. And I was frustrated with them for saying such things.

Immediately, the ambulance came and also the police came and I remember them putting me on the stretcher and the ride to the hospital and I remember trying to joke with them because they looked so grim. Then it seemed like it just all went black.

The Sad Postscript

She remained in hospitals for several months. There were several operations for skin grafts (each with a general anesthetic), numerous sessions in physical therapy, and an encounter with a hospital nun who berated her for the sin of attempting to take her own life.

She died, age 22, about three years after the immolation, a natural death in her sleep, while in a hospital being treated for the flu. Her death certificate listed the cause of death as congestive heart failure due to myocardial infarction.

Her body was shipped to her home town. Her mother had her cremated.

Ariel's Needs

What does this all add up to, in terms of Ariel Wilson's psychological needs? How do we make sense of this desperate act in terms of her own reasoning and the dispostion of her needs? As we read her account, the following needs stand out: her needs for succorance, affiliation, deference, abasement, nurturance. In short, a person yearning to be loved, willing to do almost anything for acceptance and affection. We can use a method that helps us place values on the 20 psychological needs and note how they shape Ariel's personality. What is important is seeing which needs predominate. From her own words, we detect a passive woman, aching for love and attention. When her friends do nothing when she visits them, sobbing (ostensibly to return a *toaster*), it tells her that her ties with others have been broken and that she is hopelessly alone in the world. And she even has the fantasy that the gasoline station attendent will magically read her mind and ask her why she is purchasing a gallon of gasoline. Her ignored, unrecognized, unfulfilled needs, vital for her life, become the text of her suicidal scenario.

Here are short definitions of the three psychological needs that were central to her death.

Succorance   To have one's needs gratified by the sympathetic aid of another; to be supported, sustained, guided, consoled, taken care of, protected, loved.

Deference   To admire and support a superior; to praise, honor, or eulogize another; yield to the influence of another; to emulate an exemplar.

Nurturance   To gratify the needs of another person; to feed, help, console, protect, comfort, take care of another; to nurture.

If Ariel's friends would have talked to her when she was returning the toaster—Were they drunk or on drugs? Had she done this several times before? Is her report accurate?—

and had there subsequently been the opportunity for psychotherapy, a therapist could have approached Ariel's thoughts of suicide by looking at her needs. While the therapist could not directly provide love to Ariel, he or she could have avoided being distracted by the plethora of interesting but tangential details and focused on Ariel's central need for succorance, affection, and support. The very exploration of this need could have engaged Ariel's bright and sensitive mind in a creative and life-sustaining examination of the sources and content of her overfocused, life-threatening need for love.

In Ariel, the role of psychache and the allure of the peace of the grave seem clear, but some psychological aspects are not so obvious. Her musings in the cemetery are central. In that site, she yearns for the good, neutral, solid earth, and we are reminded of Murray's discussion of *terra firma* as the core of succorance. We see her need for security in her yearnings to be loved and protected by her (flawed) parents, especially at Christmastime, and in her desires to be loved and appreciated by a husband. The basic need for succorance will not go away. She wants the peace of the deep earth, the order of Nature's cycle of life and death, the sanctuary of the great womb. And when her immolative fire is literally consuming her, it is the *noise* that surprises and upsets her. She had sought the embracing quiet of an untended grave and she felt totally betrayed by the roar of the inferno.

PART TWO

The Psychology
of Suicide

3

Clues and Constrictions:
Indirect Suicide and
Hastened Death

The single most important outcome of the psychological suicide prevention revolution that began in the 1950s at the Los Angeles Suicide Prevention Center was the finding that *clues* preceded suicide, and thus there were possible intervention strategies for prevention. Clues are observable items that precede (and, in a sense, forecast) the event in which we are mainly interested. They are precursors, indicating the approach of a dire event, like a disease or suicide or other catastrophe. The technical synonyms for these "clues," synonyms a clinician might use, include phrases like "premonitory signs" or "prodromal indices." These are events that cast their shadow before them and serve as a warning.

From the beginning of my work in suicidology, it seemed clear that there were two kinds of clues: verbal and behavioral. In general, verbal clues to suicide are statements made by any individual that can be interpreted to mean that the person is saying goodbye in some indirect, perhaps direct, way, that they will not be around in the foreseeable future. "I won't be here next year"; "This is the last time I'll be in your office"; "You won't see me again"; "I can't take it anymore." One curious paradox in suicide is that individuals *do* leave clues—perhaps as part of their deepest ambivalence between the need to stop the pain and the concomitant wish for intervention and rescue. In any event, these verbal clues are often disguised or encoded or cryptic. As we will see later in this chapter, the opposite is also true; some people who kill themselves are capable of dissembling and failing to give any overt hint of their lethal intentions. The general rule of thumb is that if someone—a patient or colleague or friend or family member—says something that is puzzling or cryptic (in regard to life and death), the best response is to ask what was meant by that remark, and then, if there is any suspicion of suicidal intent, to ask directly, "Are you talking about suicide?"

Behavioral clues to suicide present another kind of challenge for the potential rescuer. These clues are bits of behavior that any individual might engage in if he or she were going away on a long trip. They include such obvious activities as suddenly putting one's affairs in order, straightening one's files, deciding to make a will, and, especially, inexplicably giving away or returning prized possessions. Ariel's returning the toaster on a snowy night was her way of indicating that she wouldn't be needing it any more, ever. You would think that some acts would be painfully obvious, but there is an actual case in which one medical student offered to give a classmate (who had only a monocular microscope) his binocular microscope. The recipient accepted the better instrument with gratitude only to learn the following day that the donor had hanged himself the night before. A simple question such as "What is going on?" or "Why are you doing this?"—why would anyone in medical school give away a microscope?—instead of a thoughtless "Gee, thanks" might have led to disclosures that could have saved that life.

A young woman who jumped off a high balcony in a hospital (and survived to tell about it)described how she walked from one building to another on a narrow steel I-beam high above the ground dressed only in a short hospital gown,"hoping that someone would see me out of all those windows; the whole building is made of glass."

The behaviors I have mentioned are not the items usually cited for *depression*, such as disturbances in sleeping and eating. The emphasis in this book is on the psychological aspects related to the suicidal act, such as the impulse to talk about it (albeit in a coded or disguised way) and actually behaving as though one were going to be gone and would have no need for a watch, or pen, or sweater, or piece of jewelry, or toaster, or hunting gun, or microscope. How do we know all these things? These clues were discovered (in the 1950s) by conducting "psychological autopsies" of deceased people who had committed suicide.

My colleague Robert E. Litman, who for years was the chief psychiatrist at the Los Angeles Suicide Prevention Center, reminds me that the matter is not a simple one. There are two sets of data: prospective and retrospective. The prospective clues include suicidal communications, previous suicide attempts, self-destructive behaviors, death-oriented activities, feelings of hopelessness, profound depression, tumultuous stress, telephone calls to helping agencies, among others. Then there are the retrospective clues. In the psychological autopsies performed on equivocal coroner's cases, we must consider a number of elements related to suicide, including the presence of mild depression, the recent death of a loved one, unrelenting stress on the job, tension in the marriage, alcoholism, schizophrenia, physical illness, constricted or dichotomous (all-or-none) thinking, thoughts and talk of death, and so forth. Of course, the number of people who manifest such clues is enormously larger than the number who actually commit suicide. In a note to me, Litman added: "The reason suicide prevention through the use of clues to suicide has not been more successful is that clues reveal multitudes of prospectively suicidal persons and helping resources are all too limited."

On the typical death certificate (in our 50 states and most countries in the world) there is an item that reads "Accident, Suicide, Homicide." If this item is not checked, then "Natural" is implied. One of the main goals of the certification of any death is to classify the death in terms of these four *modes* of death—what I have called the NASH classification of death: Natural, Accident, Suicide, Homicide. In death, as in life, some critical matters are not always clear-cut; a sizable percentage of deaths—say, around 10 percent—are *equivocal* as to mode. This uncertainty usually devolves between two modes: Was it accident or suicide?

After the forensic and toxicological evidence is in, the answer may still not be clear. "It depends," says the certifying coroner. "On what?" you may ask. "It depends on what was in the mind of the deceased. It depends on what the dead person's *intentions* were." Whether she took those pills with the intention of sleeping and waking up, or with the intention of never waking up. But how can you find that out inasmuch as she is dead? We can ask around, talk to people who knew her, reconstruct her personality, examine her life-style especially in the days just before her death, ascertain what she said and what she did. In other words, we can conduct a psychological autopsy.

In the early 1950s, the late Dr. Theodore Curphey, then Chief Medical Exmainer-Coroner of Los Angeles County, contacted the senior staff of the then-new Suicide Prevention Center, and asked us—Drs. Norman Farberow, Robert E. Litman, and me—to consult with him on recent deaths that were equivocal or unclear as to mode of death. We were deputized and went off to meet the families, friends, and co-workers of the deceased to talk with them. We had no bias for one mode of death over another. What we wanted to do was generate psychological facts and, at the same time, assuage the grief of the principal parties. The net result of this procedure could have been predicted: Additional relevant information is always helpful. In many cases we were able to help the coroner change an equivocal certification to one mode or the other, based on persuasive evidence we had generated. And it was also evident that our efforts, far from being disruptive to the survivors, were deemed—as they expressed themselves by letter to the coroner—helpful and comforting.

In the interests of scientific inquiry we then conducted some psychological autopsies on a number of *un*equivocal suicides where there was evidence of a suicide note, gun in the hand, and so on. What we found in this series was that about 90 percent of unequivocal suicides had given verbal or behavioral clues within the week or so before they committed suicide. In the vast majority of suicide cases, the clues were there. But some questions remain: How do we reconcile the fact that most people who commit suicide give or emit clues as to their intention with the seemingly contradictory fact that most people who talk suicide do not commit it? And what about the 10 percent of people who actually commit suicide for whom no clues were found?

Most people who commit suicide talk about it; most people who talk about suicide do not commit it. Which to believe? The answer is: Both are right. They simply represent two different ways of looking at the data. These two ways are the prospective (looking forward) and the retrospective (looking backward) views. We can schematize this by using circles to represent the relevant categories. In the prospective set, the suicide circle, in terms of actual numbers, is tiny compared to the circle for clues; whereas, in the retrospective set, the circle for clues is almost as large as the circle for known committed suicides.

If one starts in the present with everyone who has threatened suicide and follows them into the future for, say, five years, happily only a small minority—about 2 or 3 percent—will commit suicide. That is the prospective view. On the other hand, if one takes a group of individuals who have actually committed suicide and attempts to ascertain how many had talked about taking their own lives, our studies (done in Los Angeles) show that about 90 percent have done so. That is the retrospective view. Given that both views are right, what we can say is that, in practice, it is the better part of wisdom to adopt the conservative (retrospective) view, and take any talk of suicide seriously. In the choice between these two sets of data, common sense tells us that it is preferable to err on the side of caution.

If about 90 percent of the people who commit suicide have given clues, what are we to make of the other 10 percent? How is it that some people who are on the verge of suicide can hide or mask their secretly held intentions? "He seemed perfectly normal" is an example of this kind of report that one often reads in the newspapers about a person who has committed suicide. We are then thrown, conceptually, into the world of *dissembling*. This is the world of individuals who keep their own secrets even, or especially, from their spouses. They are people who live undisclosed lives. We are then in the world of masks and pretense; it is the world of double lives, even of spies and secret agents; and also of quiet, laconic, and naturally taciturn people; of people who live together and seemingly love each other and still do not share their most important personal plans, such as the plan to kill themselves on the morrow.

Here is an excerpt from a contemporary personal account by the eminent writer William Styron. It relates how he, as a suicidal person, could "regard all others, the healthy and the normal, as living in parallel but separate worlds."

> My wife and I had been invited to dinner with half-a-dozen friends at a fine Italian restaurant in New York. I very much feared the hour . . . by dinnertime I felt virtually suffocated by psychic discomfort. Of course that evening I could have stayed at home [but] the anguish is lodged in the mind, so that it matters little where the corporeal self is located; one will feel equal desolation at home in one's armchair or trying to eat dinner at Primavera.
>
> I say "trying" to eat dinner, because my appetite had decreased over the previous week to the point where I was eating purely for sustenance. Two of my table companions were charming friends I had known for years. I had picked [at my food] without tasting it. For no particular reason, the sense of encroaching doom was especially powerful that night. But the demented stoicism . . . caused me to register scarcely a flicker of this inner devastation. I chatted with my companions, nodded amiably, made the appropriate frowns and smiles.
>
> The restroom was nearby down a flight of carpeted stairs. On the way there the fantasies of suicide, which had been embedded in my thoughts daily for several weeks and which I had kept at bay during the dinner conversation, returned

in a flood. To rid myself of this torment (but how? and when?) becomes the paramount need. . . . I wondered desperately if I could make it through the rest of the evening without betraying my condition. On my return to the floor above I astonished myself by expressing my misery aloud in a spontaneous utterance which my normal self would have rejected in shame. "I'm dying," I groaned, to the obvious dismay of a man passing down the stairway. The blurted words were one of the most fearsome auguries of my will to self-destruction; within a week I would be writing, in a stupor of disbelief, suicide notes.

Some months later . . . my two table companions reflected that I had appeared to be behaving quite normally. The monumental aplomb I exhibited is testimony to the almost uniquely interior nature of the pain . . . a pain that is all but indescribable, and therefore to anyone but the sufferer almost meaningless.[1]

It is almost as though the suicidal drama were autonomously writing itself, as though the *play* had a mind of its own. It has to sober us to realize that as long as people, consciously or unconsciously, can successfully dissemble, no suicide prevention program can be 100 percent successful.

We can understand this dissembling in psychological terms, and see it as much more than feigning or malingering. This is so because there is at least a touch of schizophrenia or insanity in every suicide in the sense that, in suicide, there is *some* disconnection between thoughts and feelings. The current psychiatric term for this condition is "alexithymia," by which is meant the presence of conscious and apparent psychic suffering characterized by sadness, gloominess, despair, or despondency, and accompanied by the inability to connect emotional experiences with thoughts. This results in an impaired ability to label emotions, or to differentiate them into more subtle shades of meaning, and communicate them to others. It is this abnormal "split" between what we think and what we feel. There lies the illusion of control; there lies madness. When we are in a normal mood we experience the thoughts and feelings together, as one unified conscious moment. In the suicidal person, the death-laden *thoughts* are so singularly dangerous because they lack the gyroscopic balance of sufficient positive emotions.

There is, however, one undissemblable sign that almost never can be hidden, an aspect of mental life and behavior that is characteristic of the suicidal state of mind. It is called *constriction*, and refers to a narrowing or tunneling of the focus of attention. It comes out especially in the ordinary speech of the potentially suicidal person, in the use of certain words that reflect the all-or-nothing (dichotomous) thinking of the pre-suicidal mind.

The single most dangerous word in all of suicidology is the four-letter word *only*—as in this brief excerpt from the words of a young woman who jumped from a high place and just luckily survived. (Count the number of times the word *only* appears.)

> I was so desperate. I felt, my God, I can't face this thing. Everything was like a terrible whirlpool of confusion. And I thought to myself, there's only one thing to do. I just have to lose consciousness. That's the only way to get away from it. And the only way to lose consciousness, I thought, was to jump off something good and high.

Later in her account she tells us:

> And then I got to the fifth floor and everything just got very dark all of a sudden, and all I could see was this balcony. Everything around it just blacked out. It was just like a circle. That was all I could see. Just the balcony. And I climbed over it and just let go. I was so desperate.

In her chilling description of constriction, she evokes the image of the diaphragm of a camera closing down on its tightest focus. In suicide, the diaphragm of the mind narrows and focuses on the single goal of escape to the exclusion of all else—parents, spouse, children. Those other persons in the life are not forgotten; they are simply not within the narrow focus of the suicidal lens. Suddenly they are just not in the picture.

A. Alvarez, the English writer and critic—and a self-described failed suicide—in his first-rate book on suicide, *The Savage God* (1972), described this "closed world of suicide":

> Once a man decides to take his own life he enters a shut-off, impregnable but wholly convincing world where every detail fits and every incident reinforces his decision. Each of these deaths has its own inner logic and unrepeatable despair.[2]

Another author, Boris Pasternak, wrote about the suicidal constriction of several young Russian poets who had been persecuted by the Stalinist regime:

> A young man who decides to commit suicide puts a full stop to his being, he turns his back on his past, and declares himself bankrupt and his memories to be unreal. They can no longer help or save him; he has put himself beyond their reach. The continuity of his inner life is broken, and his personality is at an end. And perhaps what finally makes him kill himself is not the firmness of his resolve but the unbearable quality of this anguish which belongs to no one, of this suffering in the absence of the sufferer, which is empty because his life has stopped and he can no longer feel it.[3]

One of the first tasks of any aspiring helper or therapist with a highly suicidal person is to address the constriction, to "widen the blinders," to let some light in so that the person can see new angles. And, as we will see, the therapist must gently disagree with the death-laden premises of the suicidal person. The suicidal person's thinking pattern has constricted; often it is dichotomous with only two possibilities: yes or no, life as I want it or death, my way or nothing, greatness or annihilation—the desperation of seeing only two alternatives, and not three or more choices as we do in ordinary life. In the camera of the mind, the suicidal film is limited to stark black and white.

I recall a college student who had told a friend that she had purchased a revolver with the sole intention of killing herself. The friend encouraged her to see me at my university office. The student was 20, single, attractive, demure, well-to-do, and filled with Victorian sensibilities; she had had sexual intercourse once in her life a few months before, and was pregnant. She told me (in the language of the unconscious) that she "couldn't bear to live." The choice she presented to me was that she somehow had to be unpregnant—to turn the clock back to before the fateful night—or dead. A punishing dichotomy for her—impossible to fulfill. At that moment, given those two choices, suicide seemed her *only* option.

I did several things. For one, I took out a legal pad of paper and began, with her reluctant help, to generate a list—"Shneidman's lousy list," I called it. Our exchange went something like this: "You could bring the child to term and keep it." ("I couldn't do that.") "You could bring the child to term and put it up for adoption." ("I can't do that.") "You could have an abortion here locally." (I'm not going to do that.") "You could go away and have an abortion." ("Not that.") "You could involve your parents." ("I won't do that.") "You could talk to the young man involved." ("I definitely won't do that.") "And you can always commit suicide, but there is no reason to do that today." (No comment by her.) The won'ts, the can'ts, the have-to's, the must's, the never's, the always's—the person's initial unnegotiables—these are the main topics of therapy. "Now," I said, "let's look at our list, and would you please rank order them from the absolutely least acceptable on up to the least distasteful."

The very making of this list, the nonjudgmental attitude, had already had a calming effect on her. We had broken the dichotomy and enlarged her view. She actually ranked the list, mumbling dissent at each item. But what was of critical importance was that suicide was no longer a first or second choice. She put a "1" and a "2" with some tears, but when she wrote "3," I knew that her life was saved and we were then simply haggling about life—which is a perfectly viable state, and for some people, at least at some times, the normal state of affairs.

It was possible to achieve the assignment of the moment—to loosen this young woman's suicidal resolve by reducing her confusion, her shame, and her panic, and by widening her constricted perception of her range of options. Her original dichotomous choice involving only suicide gave way to some viable choices within the scope of life's realistic options. There was now some hope.

I also did a number of practical things on her behalf, including making some telephone calls (in her presence), to set in motion what she had chosen as the least-undesirable-choice-under-these-circumstances; the reasonably best that one could do. She could live with that. And, who knows, a suicide was possibly prevented.

There are many ways to shorten your life other than committing suicide. We can call these cases of indirect suicide.

What are we to make of people who act as though they were afraid they were going to be late to their own accidents, who foolishly disregard a lifesaving medical regimen, who use bad judgment to shorten or truncate their lives, who seem set on premature self-destruction, who imprudently put themselves in harm's way, who seem bent on covert self-destruction, whose health habits are known to jeopardize life, who appear to be their own worst enemies? What comes to mind, by way of understanding, are ideas like *in*direct suicide and *sub*intentioned death.

We hear a lot about being "All that you can be," savoring life, self-actualizating yourself, aspiring to peak experiences. But on the negative side, there are two obvious deleterious things we can do to ourselves: We can shorten life's length, and we can narrow life's breadth. Make it shorter than it need be, or make it less than it ought to be—a narrow, pinched, and unhappy life.

Karl Menninger was the grandfather of American suicidology. In his widely read and much admired books he alerted us to the undeniable *unconscious* element in covert human self-destruction. Menninger wrote about the not-so-obvious substitutes for overt suicide. The table of contents of his seminal book *Man against Himself* reflects the topics of his interests and concerns: "Chronic Suicide"—including asceticism, martyrdom, neurotic invalidism, alcohol addiction, antisocial behavior, and psychosis; "Focal Suicide"—including self-mutilation, malingering, polysurgery, and psychologically laden accidents; and "Organic Suicide"—concerning the psychological factors in organic disease.[4] All these, said Menninger, are subtle ways in which the individual can shorten or truncate life, be less than he or she could have been; shun life's warmth and light; race toward withdrawal and self-abnegation. All of them, in his view, are partial deaths; all manifestations of indirect suicide—what I have called subintentioned deaths.

I knew and inordinately admired Dr. Karl, but my personal mentor and the hero of my intellectual life was Henry

A. Murray, professor at Harvard, with whom I studied and whom I unabashedly revered. Once, at my invitation, Dr. Murray came to Los Angeles to deliver an address that he called "Dead to the World."[5] In that presentation, he mused about partial deaths and indirect suicide:

> [I was reminded of] other related conditions, such as a temporary or permanent cessation of a part of psychic life—the cessation of affect (feeling almost dead), for example—or the cessation of an orientation of conscious life—the cessation of social life (dead to the outer world) or the cessation of spiritual life (dead to the inner world), for example—or [of] the cessation of different degrees of life—near-cessation (as good as dead) or a trend toward cessation (diminution).

Every death in the world can be identified in two important ways: (1) By one or more of a large number of *causes* (e.g., congestive heart failure, cancer, pneumonia, etc.), taken from a book called *Manual of the International Statistical Classifications of Diseases, Injuries, and Causes of Death*; and (2) in terms of one of four *modes* of death: Natural, Accident, Suicide, Homicide. In most cases, the cause of death implies the mode of death: congestive heart failure implies a natural death; crushing injuries to the chest behind a steering wheel implies an accidental death; gunshot wound to the right temple (and a note found nearby) implies a suicidal death; and gunshot wound to the back of the head implies a homicidal death.

While the cause can almost always be clearly ascertained, the mode of death may remain unclear or equivocal, sometimes forever. To the survivors, the mode of death is enormously important, not only in terms of practical matters like insurance monies and the probate of wills, but in terms of the reputation, the memory of the deceased, and all the psychological and spiritual issues related to grief and mourning.

But mode of death is too neat, too simplistic, in its categorization, leaving out the role, the intention of the deceased person in his or her own death. Did the dead person really intend it? That would be suicide. Or did the event (e.g., a commercial airplane crash) simply happen to the person? That would be accident. *Or*, did the deceased play an unconscious, indirect, covert role in effecting the demise, bringing the death-date forward? If so, that would be a *subintentioned* death.

It is obvious that many "accidents" are not entirely accidental in the sense of being fortuitous or related entirely to blind chance visited on the victim from "without." It is also clear that some homicides are unconsciously invited. Many so-called natural deaths indeed occur when they happen by virtue of specific behaviors (and misbehaviors). Not all deaths have this subintentioned quality, but a sizable percentage do.

Some years ago, the Coroner of Marin County (in northern California) and I conducted a little experiment. For a two-year period, all the coroner's cases in that county (974 cases, to be exact)—natural, accident, suicide, and homicide—were also rated as high, medium, low, and absent "lethality" on the part of the deceased. The 131 suicidal deaths were, by definition, rated as having high lethality, of being intentional. Of the remaining 843 cases, 4 were rated as having high lethality and 128 of medium lethality. In other words, 16 percent of the certified natural, accidental, and homicidal deaths were deemed to have had *some* participative element to them. This is one-sixth of all the deaths in that county. If we then extrapolate to the whole country, that would imply that there are millions of subintentioned deaths each year, in which the deceased has played some unconscious role in hastening the death-date.

But everybody already knows this startling fact; that is what the public health campaigns in relation to smoking, drug abuse, maternal care, unprotected sex, street violence, and other death-laden activities of contemporary life, especially in urban environments, are all about. The great social debate—really about subintentioned deaths—is over the role of the larger society in contributing to poverty, social degradation, and hopelessness—conditions that are clearly about behaviors that bring death to far too many victims before they need have died.

4

The Need to Strike First: The Case of Beatrice Bessen

was intrigued by a colleague's request: Would I please see and evaluate a patient of his, a young woman, even though she was almost immediately leaving the city to return to college. And so I met Beatrice Bessen—an attractive, slender, handsomely dressed young woman. A most interesting person. Not hostile, but deeply rebellious; not iconoclastic, but thoroughly unimpressed by authority; not surly, but beyond being captivated by anyone. I asked her there, in my office, to complete a Psychological Pain Questionnaire. When she handed me the completed form I saw immediately—as the reader can see in Appendix A—that here was a person who really hurt. She had rated the intensity of her psychological

pain as an 8 on a 1 to 9 scale. She had attempted suicide.
She had a great need for order, sanctuary, and a world she
could count on. But mostly what came through was her intense need, born out of fear and anxiety, to reject others
before they might possibly reject her. She was a prototypical,
although rare, case of being distressed primarily by her need
for counteraction.

Before I continue with Beatrice, I want to spread all the
needs on the table as they relate to suicide. As we saw in
Chapter 2, Ariel's psychological pain was driven primarily by
her need for succorance, to be loved. Beatrice's pain, as we
have just noted, is motivated in quite a different way. Castro
Reyes (presented in Chapter 6), has yet another disposition
of needs.

What psychological needs, then, are most often directly
related to suicide? The best general answer is that suicide is
not so much tied to the content of the need as it is to the
intensity of the frustration of whatever need is basic in the
functioning of that personality. And, of course, there is almost always more than one need involved—but I do not
wish to complicate this presentation with multiple needs and
combinations of needs. So, I have, for the sake of presenting
the overall idea, characterized each of the three cases by
their single dominant, most obvious need, around which the
frustration is clustered. On theoretical grounds, there is not
this or that need that causes suicide; it is the frustration, the
thwarting, the blocking, the incompleteness, the tension over
the fulfilling of that need, deemed important by that person,
that causes the unbearable tension.

And so Beatrice went back to college, with the promise
of writing me a rather lengthy autobiography. By that time,
I had some rather clear impressions of her personality. My
primary task was to give some assessment consultation to her
therapist—which I did.

Beatrice's skewed perceptions of her parents began before she was 10 years old, when she saw them as headed for divorce. In her eyes, they suddenly became untrustworthy and not dependable. She extrapolated from this insight into a general view of the world as dangerously unreliable. What is special about Beatrice is that she took the initiative, by way of counteraction, of rejecting her family before they could abandon her—a worst-case scenario of a self-fulfilling prophecy. What happened to her was a kind of psychological orphanhood, with the special twist of its being a self-inflicted one. And then a chronic tragic pattern developed and, once used, she could not disabuse herself of these maladaptive beliefs. This unhappy psychodynamic pattern became converted into an eating disorder in which she turned her basic distrust (hostility) of her mother and father (and their union to each other) into an unmanageable disaffection toward herself.

Counteraction is an interesting constellation of basic psychological needs not often seen. It is defined by Murray, in *Explorations in Personality* (1938), as follows:

To master or make up for a failure by restriving. To obliterate a humiliation or rejection by resumed (or increased) action. To overpower weakness; to repress fear; to efface an insult by action; to maintain self-respect and pride on a high level. Counteraction is related to the need for Achievement and the need for Inviolacy (to have one's own psychological space uninvaded). There is determination to overcome; pride; autonomy; zest for striving. Such a person is resolute, determined, indomitable, dauntless, dogged, adventurous; to make efforts, however disguised, to deal successfully with a formerly traumatic situation; to avenge a rejection; to do forbidden things just to prove they can be done; to engage in activities so as not to be scorned as inexperienced.[1]

Such a person would answer the following statements affirmatively: "I try to work out things for myself when I am in trouble; When I get bad news I hide what I feel, as if I didn't care; I go out to meet trouble rather than try to escape it; Sometimes I feel that I must do everything myself; I dislike it when I am asked about my health or my frame of mind; I would rather go without something than ask a favor; I am determined to conquer my fears and weaknesses by myself."

Beatrice's actions were not exactly *counter*actions; they were anticipatory rather than reflexive. They were *pro*active. She did not strike back so much as she struck first. She was like a wartime commander who launches a preemptive strike; she beats the enemy to the punch. We do not know how much of this was realistically necessary when she was 8 and 10, and how much of it simply exacerbated the situation. We do know that it rendered her unhappy and launched her on a suicidal career. In any event, what we have here can be understood in large part in terms of her exaggerated and distorted need for proaction; to reject others before the "others" might or might not have rejected her.

In her childhood, after age 10, her basic unspoken syllogism went something like this:

- *Major premise*   I must find someone in this world I can totally depend on.

- *Minor premise*   I can't count on my mother or my father, either individually or collectively.

- *Conclusion*   Therefore, alas, I must depend primarily on myself. As part of this maneuver, I must actively disaffiliate from my parents. It is better to abandon them before they abandon me; to do unto others *before* they do things to me. That

leaves only me and my body. My body is part
friend, part enemy-parent. I can try to control
myself (and others) through controlling my body.
My body is my only practical handle on the world,
a rheostat (that I can turn up and turn down)—gain
or lose the same 15 pounds—I can control my life
by controling my body. And if life gets too
painful—I can turn it off entirely.

Several months after our first meeting, during college
break, I saw Beatrice again and, on that occasion, administered Murray's Thematic Apperception Test (the TAT,
1935). The TAT consists entirely of a set of photographs,
typically of two people; the social-psychological situation is
not quite clear. The subject's task is to tell a story, relating
what the characters are thinking, feeling, and doing, and how
the whole thing turns out.

Murray had said that the TAT "is based on the well-
recognized fact that when someone attempts to interpret a
complex social situation he is apt to tell as much about himself as he is about the phenomena on which attention is
focused. To one with 'double hearing,' however, he is exposing certain inner forces and arrangements—wishes, fears,
as well as conscious and unconscious expressions of his experiences and fantasies."[2] In other words, the TAT allows
the person to project his or her unconscious perceptual
styles or habitual ways of "looking at the world."

Here is Beatrice's response to a TAT card in which a
young boy is contemplating a violin that rests on a table in
front of him.

It's a picture of a little boy. And it seems like he's missing
something. Someone. Like he's being reminded of some-

thing about this violin. He's being reminded looking at this violin in front of him. Maybe he's missing the person who used to play the violin. A friend, or teacher or parents, or another sibling. He just is looking at the violin and missing the player of it and eventually he'll get up and go on about his day. It is a reminder of somebody, because they are no longer playing the music.

My private thoughts (and what I shared with her therapist) were that here is a story with a remarkably idiosyncratic twist: A singular focus on the people who are *not* in the picture; the presence of the absent. There is a yearning and a sense of loss for what (and who) are not in her life. It has a sad and poignant tone. The key word is "missing." The child in the story has been abandoned; the teller of the story is psychologically bereft.

Another TAT card shows a young man sitting opposite an older man who looks as though he were emphasizing some point in an argument. Here is the story Beatrice told:

Two men are listening to a story that is being told to them by someone who is not in the picture. The younger man is looking intently at the person who is telling the story, listening very hard, and the older man is looking at him, looking for his reaction, a facial reaction, to the story. Perhaps he already knows the story. Maybe it's this man's wife and he knows what she is going to say, and he's looking for the young man's reaction.

My inner comments: Yet again, a main character "is not in the picture"—off camera, in the wings, not *directly* available. There is a curious notion of searching people's faces for clues; a sense of being lost, of not feeling sure of what the standards are. This story reenforces the off-beat, aberrant tone of her perceptual style.

At our third meeting, six months after the previous one,

she delivered her searing autobiographic life story. Here it is, entirely (except for a few words) in her own words.

My childhood was fine, growing up in the suburbs which were relatively safe then. I had self-confidence like most children do. My memory becomes rather intense at the age of 10. I remember knowing, somehow, that my parents were going to divorce someday, and so I began to read books about children of divorced parents. When I told my mom how I felt she said they had no plans to divorce. Three years later my mom moved out of the house.

At age 10 I sort of "woke up" to the horrors of the world. I came out of my childhood innocence and dove head-first into the dark side of life. Recognizing that I was vulnerable to severe pain, and predicting my household was breaking up, I began to pull away from my family. By the time my mom and dad came out of their denial, I had distanced myself enough that the impact of their separation didn't effect me. My older brother cried, and I simply thought he was being weak. I submerged myself in my friends, having discounted my family's ability to support me.

The divorce proceedings began as I entered high school, and continued for two very ugly years as my parents fought like children over alimony and retirement funds. In high school, I was given more opportunities to escape my "family" life (I had begun using the term "family" as loosely as possible, since my friends were my true family, and my family just blood relatives). I joined the theater arts department and a rock n' roll band.

I had secretly wanted to live with my father, but couldn't hurt my mother's feelings. Unfortunately, my father leaned on me too strongly and confessed to me his thoughts of suicide and his increasing abuse of alcohol. I listened, thinking he was doing me a favor by confiding in me, and carried around an impossible load of guilt and sadness for my father's state of mind.

High school had its highlights, but it wasn't enough to distract me from my growing self-hate. At age 15 I was struggling with my feelings and did not understand what was happening to me. I remember trying to explain it to my friends, who shook their heads in disbelief at my descriptions of falling in a black hole and my declarations that life was meaningless, but they simply could not relate to my morbid thoughts.

Once I realized I was alone in my thoughts, I stopped talking about them. I was terrified that I was insane and didn't want anyone to find out, so I continued to mimic the behaviors of my "normal" friends and put on a smile everywhere I went. That same year my brother moved out and went out of the state to college, leaving me with the fragmented mess known as our family. I still resent his narrow escape from the daily hell that followed in his absence. I heard everything.

At this point, although I was rarely at either parent's house, I needed something to distract myself from the burden of their bickering. The answer was handed to me by a teenage boy I was dating and thought I "loved." He told me that I needed to lose five pounds. I believed him, anxious to find a reason why I was so unhappy. At 5 feet 4 and 120 pounds I went on a diet. The diet gave me many of the things I craved: Attention, control, self-confidence, and order. Little did I know that I would end up with an eating disorder that haunts me to this day.

The boyfriend who began my descent into anorexia chose the following week to break up with me. He abruptly broke up with me. I could not handle the overflowing waves of pain that washed through my body immediately after the breakup. I had never felt such intense pain and I could not handle it. I was alone at home and ran desperately around, panicked over the flood of emotions that was traveling through my body. I ended up taking the kitchen knife into my room and cutting myself, slashes all along my arms. The physical pain let me pull my attention off the emotional agony, and I just concentrated on not letting the blood spill over onto the carpet. That day I clearly remember wanting to die.

In retrospect, that day was a catalyst for a speedy downward spiral that engulfed the rest of my adolescence. I was able to maintain a "false self" at school and in my activities. For the next two years, no one, even my close friends, knew how I felt inside. Every night, before fading off to sleep, I imagined committing suicide. I became obsessed with death. I rehearsed my own funeral over and over, adding careful details each time. I listened to a genre of music known as "gothic" which had dark, murky tunes to accompany tragic lyrics of loss and death. I began to write poetry questioning existence, God, human intentions, and philosophy. But nothing gave me relief. I became more and more cynical about the daily task of living, and distanced myself further from my emotions. After a while, I was completely numb.

I used my excessive discipline to deprive myself of food and comfort. I felt I needed to "suffer" in order to "deserve" the right to walk down the street. I used drugs, ditched school, and slept overnight in my car (telling whichever parent that I was at a friend's house). I managed to maintain an impossibly low weight for the summer before my senior year of high school. The bad mood had taken over. I described it then as a monster that was bigger than I was. I was tired, very tired, and I gave in to it.

Though I had considered suicide for a long time, I had not made a serious attempt yet. After working on a plan for three months, I tried to kill myself a week before my seventeenth birthday. In my beloved car, at 2 A.M. on a rainy night, I slit my wrists with a newly purchased, large exacto knife. I had already prepared an audiotape (I felt that a suicide note was too commonplace and wanted to be original) and I left copies of it at the door of two close friends. I was ready to die.

I know now that slitting my wrists was not as poetic nor as easy as I had imagined. Due to blood clotting and fainting, it is actually difficult to die from such wounds. The evening dragged on with me busy reopening the stubborn veins that insisted upon clotting up. I was patient and persistent, thinking of myself as a mad surgeon with scalpel in hand, and cut away at myself for over an hour. The battle with my body to die was unexpected, and after waging a good fight, I passed out.

I awoke, to my disappointment, in my car. I was still myself, still alive, and still in pain. Nothing had changed except that my wrists felt drained and raw. I didn't know what to do. I started up in my car in a daze and drove blindly, hardly able to use my arms to steer the car to a place which was near my designated gravesite.

I spent the following three days in my car, in shock. I hardly remember that period of time. I used my last two dollars for French fries at a nearby drive-through. I had no change of clothes and no way to hide the dried blood, so I remained in my car, just sitting. But mostly, I didn't think at all.

I decided to drive back near home to ask one of my close friends for advice on what to do next. He had tried to hang himself a year before and I figured he might be able to help me. I wanted to take a shower before seeing him, so I thought I would just stop by my father's house and use the bathroom. It never occurred to me that my dad wouldn't be at work. When I approached the house on foot and saw his car, I turned and walked quickly away, surprised that he was home.

At that moment, my father, somehow, glanced out of the front window. He ran out and rushed over to me. I was sure I was going to be sent to jail. Instead, a bag of clothes was packed, a few more phone calls were made, and I was taken to a mental hospital.

I spent three and a half months locked indoors on an adolescent psychiatric unit. I met other kids who felt the way I did. I was introduced to a million therapies. And I attempted suicide again in my tiny room after smashing a light bulb and using the glass to slice my veins open. Yet the overall experience was a positive one. I was removed from my "family" environment long enough to gain some perspective on my situation, and I connected with others who felt as desperate as I did. However, I was not "cured." I was released from the hospital AMA (against medical advice) because my father was fed up with the high costs and the pop psychology suggestions of the institution. The day after I was out, I went on my first real eating binge, devouring my father's kitchen contents after months of hospital food. The following day I resolved to diet once again.

Although I was feeling better, the underlying causes of my unhappiness had yet to be tackled. I no longer spent my evenings planning my funeral; instead, I prepared the following day's menu and exercise regimen. I spent the last semester of my senior year (having kept up with my classmates by using the hospital's school program) alternately dieting and binging. I lost and gained the same fifteen pounds a hundred times.

Going away to college at age 18 was a wise choice for me. Escaping from the chaos of my home life, as well as the confusion of a big city, helped me quite a bit. I slowly made new friends. Of course, it wasn't perfect. My eating disorder took on new shapes, resulting in heavy laxative abuse and binging during my first two years of college and strict dieting and severe weight loss during my final two years. I attended a support group for bulimia and anorexia, but never entered one-on-one therapy, having feared no real solution after my experience with intensive therapy in the hospital.

During my fairly peaceful college years, suicide still played a role. Most obvious was my eating disorder, which on some level was an attempt to slowly end my life. Less obvious was my disturbingly dark poetry, and my instant thought of suicide each time a difficult problem would arise. I simply kept suicide in the back of my mind as an option. It made me feel safer. My sick logic hadn't changed since adolescence.

During my junior year, my rich college friends took their year abroad, leaving me alone at school. I thought of suicide over and over. I ate next to nothing and slept all the time. Finally, I told my mother I was suicidal again and she, after threatening hospitalization, suggested I see a psychiatrist. I walked out of his office with a prescription for Prozac.

Prozac was a mini-miracle for me. I had abused drugs on and off since I was 16 and I felt excited about swallowing the tiny green and white pill each morning. I hoped this was my "cure," my savior from all this pain. I was a perfect candidate for Prozac, especially since one of the few side effects was appetite suppression. The psychiatrist was right, surprise, surprise! Twenty milligrams a day and I could attend classes, meet new people, skip more meals, and not lock myself up in my room all day. I made new friends and didn't think about suicide any more. I did, however, over the course of five months lose a tremendous amount of weight and was diagnosed with anorexia nervosa by a campus physician. Still on Prozac, and still dealing with anorexia today, I am no longer feeling the euphoria I was promised for two dollars a pill.

My final year of college was the best one. My anorexia was manageable and my spirits lifted enough to enjoy life. I even allowed myself a few months thinking I was "cured" and that the pain of the past decade was finally over. But as graduation approached, I started sleeping more and eating less. I was definitely coming down from a year-long high.

I have now graduated from college. I moved back home, am living with my father, and was rehired at last year's summer job for the whole year. I have been accepted into graduate school but I am deferring that for one year. I have recently realized that I do not want to spend the rest of my life sliding up and down the scale of mental illness. I need to address those things that were never dealt with in the hospital.

Even though I am scared and rather reluctant to take a year off my neatly packaged future, there is a part of me screaming for help. I cannot ignore this plea. My anorexia has grown much worse since I've been home, and I know my health is in danger. For me, restricting my food intake is not about being fashionably thin, it's about my death wish that has actually never left me.

Although it is normal for college graduates to question who they are, and where they are going, my emotional turmoil does not allow for a "normal" contemplative time. While my friends complain, cry a little, get frustrated and confused a little, I try to talk myself into starving to death. My logic allows for this, once again, because I still fear that I cannot handle the floods of pain that I expect are waiting for me beneath my psyche. In many ways I am still that 15 year old racing about the house searching for a way out of such extreme pain. And my impulse still is to grab the closest knife and begin cutting.

From the beginning, I thought of Beatrice in terms of the disposition of her psychological needs, and assessed her with these ideas in mind. The needs I rated highest are counteraction, autonomy, inviolacy, and understanding. These reflect her rather independent, isolated, feisty, spirited personality.

Taken together, these four needs give Beatrice a certain flavor. No one would confuse her with Ariel, the young immolator. The interactions with these two women would obviously be somewhat different. I have left for Part Four how psychotherapy with each of these young women might have proceeded.

Beatrice has been in an almost lifetime war against her

parents. Unfortunately, the suit of armor she built against adults turned out to be mostly a hair shirt. The last stanza of Elder Olson's poem, "Directions to the Armorer"—which I shared with her therapist—comes to mind.

> Make the armor itself
> As tough as possible,
> But on a reverse
> Principle; don't
> Worry about its
> Saving my hide;
> Just fix it to give me
> Some sort of protection—
> Any sort of protection—
> From a possible enemy
> Inside.[3]

She once mentioned her cats, special breeds, with whom she has a close and non-counteractive relationship. "There is nothing," she told me, "like one's purring cat."

PART THREE

Aspects
of Suicide

5

Suicidal Life Histories

Facts alone can be very interesting. But sometimes their implications seem much more imperative. Earlier in my career, in 1969—the year I was a Fellow at the Center for the Advanced Study in the Behavioral Sciences (on the Stanford campus)—I surprised myself by identifying five suicides from among a group of 30 men several years before the suicides actually occurred. That fact, while eye-catching in itself, had, in my mind, a number of provocative implications. If suicide can be identified several years before it happens, does this mean that suicide is embedded in the life history? Are individuals star-crossed and unable to change their own fates? Is suicide in the character, "bred in the bone"? Is one's life history immutable? To what extent is it malleable? Can things be done to prevent suicide? And, if so, why were things not done in those cases?

My inquiries in 1969 at Stanford were a very small part of a much larger, world-famous study usually referred to as the Terman Study of the Gifted. It is the story of Lewis M. Terman (1877–1956). Before World War I, Terman, then already a Professor of Psychology at Stanford, translated French intelligence tests, and standardized them for American children. The test, ready in 1916, was called the Stanford-Binet Intelligence Scale. It introduced the concept of the intelligence quotient (IQ)—"mental age" divided by chronological age—and was, for years, the most widely used psychometric test in America.

Terman's own interests became more focused on children with high IQs, the bright and gifted kids. He wondered: What are these children like? And what becomes of them as adults, and through their lives?

In 1921, Terman and his group began a major study. They asked teachers in California to nominate their brightest first-grade children. They tested the children, and those with IQs above 140—the top 1 percent—were then selected to be part of this ongoing, longitudinal study; 1,528 children, about equally divided between boys and girls, were selected. Parents, teachers, and the subjects themselves were interviewed over the years. At regular intervals, questionnaires were elicited from the cooperative subjects. A series of important books—with the weighty title of *Genetic Studies of Genius*— was published by the Stanford University Press.[1] The study continues to this day, with the survivors who are now mostly in their eighties. The number has dwindled to just several hundred, but the study is remarkable, even among the few longitudinal studies in the world, for the loyalty of its subjects.

When Terman began the study in the 1920s, the prevailing notion (in the public mind and even among educators) was that very bright children were, by and large, sickly, maladjusted, and eccentric—"neurotic," you might say. Terman's impeccable empirical findings showed just the opposite. The *data* for the bright children showed that they tend to be taller, healthier, better developed, and social leaders. The human organism is a whole. When genes and fortune are bountiful and give a lucky individual a better brain, they also tend to give that person a better skeleton and a better heart. Terman's findings changed all of pedogogical thinking about gifted children—and resulted in enriched curricula, special schools, among other things, and more respect all around. An unusual mind, a vigorous body, and a well-adjusted personality are perfectly compatible.

The gifted children also did well as adults. There was not a genius (at the level of Da Vinci, Newton, Darwin, Russell, or Einstein) in the group, but they did provide a disproportionately large number of judges, doctors, professors, deans, writers, business executives, and Hollywood (non-actor) luminaries for a couple of generations of California culture. They fill *Who's Who* and many are very well known, but none is *world* famous.

Importantly, as an adult group, there was almost no insanity, a lower (compared to the general population their age) divorce rate, a lower rate of alcoholism, and fewer neuropsychiatric hospitalizations and other indications of acute psychological or social distress. Among the 1,528 persons, there was only one felony arrest, and that for white-collar embezzlement. The mortality rate was lower—that is, there was a higher percentage of Terman subjects alive at various ages than in the matched general population. There were, however, more suicides than in the general population; by 1970 there were 28 known suicides among the 1,528 people, a rate obviously higher than that of the 12 per 100,000 in the general population.

In 1969, through the help of Professor Robert Sears, arrangements were made for me to have access to the confidential Terman Study research records. Professor Sears—himself a Terman subject—was then scientific co-executor of the Terman Study. (This relationship has continued, after Dr. Sears's death in 1987, with Professor Albert Hastdorf.) Among the 28 suicidal deaths, there was a group of five men who had, within a two-year period, committed suicide, all by gunshot, all around age 55. I decided to study each individual of this small subgroup intensively. The plan was that I would study 30 matched cases—15 still alive, 10 dead from natural causes, and the 5 suicides—but with everything in the record after 1964, five years before, deleted. Each set of folders was edited so that I could not tell if the individual was dead or alive. The cases came to me, one at a time, in random order. Essentially what I did was to create a lengthy life chart (following the teachings of Adolf Meyer) for each person—reams of typed material for each individual, with dates, and columns for events that were going on concomitantly—and then I mused and thought about each life. In each case, I examined the life more or less chronologically, attempting to order the materials and keep in mind a number of related skeins. I got to know each man fairly well—entirely through the records, of course. I made continuous ratings, in my mind and in notes, of the individual's ongoing perturbation and lethality as he moved through his life.

At the end of a year's work (and before I left the Center to go to UCLA), I wrote a memorandum to Professor Sears:

> My analysis of the data and possibly the data themselves do not permit me to state with anything like full confidence which five cases were suicidal. The best that I can do—from

my subjective ratings of each individual's perturbation and
lethality—is to rank order 11 of the cases as the most likely
candidates for suicidal status. I should be somewhat surprised if any of the other 19 individuals committed suicide.
The rank order follows: . . .

The facts revealed that the individual I had ranked as
number 1 had, in fact, committed suicide, my number 2
committed suicide, number 3 was living, numbers 4, 5 and
6 had committed suicide. Numbers 7 and 9 were living; and
8, 10, and 11 had died natural deaths. The statistical prob-
ability of choosing four of five suicidal cases by chance alone
is 1 out of 1,131. Obviously, there are discernible clues in
case history materials, if one looks hard enough.

One striking finding was that the patterns of life consistent
with a suicidal outcome at age 55 were discernible to me—
on the basis of my working notes—by the time the person
was in his *late twenties*. Before I present an explication of
these life clues, here is a tight summary of my clinical impression of what seemed to characterize these five suicides:
The *father*, even in his absence, *starts* the life course to
suicide, *school* and *work* (and the feelings of inferiority and
chronic *hopelessness*) *exacerbate* it, and the *spouse* can either
aid the *rescue* from it or play a *precipitating* role in effecting
suicide.

Here is what the clues looked like in the records.[2]

Early childhood clues   In general, for the suicidal cases,
the relationships with the father turned out to be more critical than relationships with the mother, and these relationships were painful or strained and had a sense of (obvious
or subtle) rejection in them. There is a note from the teacher
about this 14-year-old bright boy (who killed himself at
55)—whose father owned an enormous furniture manufac-
turing business. "This boy's parents are of two minds: his

mother is for college, his father thinks that college is of no value to a person who expects to take up the business. The boy does not show very much hard-mindedness. His type is more the theoretical. He prefers ideas to matter." In a subsequent letter to Professor Terman, his father called his son "stupid."

Least successful subjects   In 1968, a member of the Terman Study staff, Melita Oden, wrote a monograph on 100 of the Terman subjects ranked as most successful and 100 matched subjects rated as least successful. Three of the five suicides were in the least successful group; none in the most successful. Subsequently, I did a separate study of a subgroup of Terman Study lawyers, in which experts assigned adjectives to the life histories of Terman Study lawyers, independently rated as most successful and least successful. The words (or trait-labels) ascribed to the *most* successful lawyers were: ambitious, capable, competitive, conscientious, contented, fair-minded, intelligent, outgoing, reasonable, responsible, secure, self-controlled, sincere, and sophisticated. The trait-labels ascribed to the *least* successful lawyers were: cautious, conscientious, defensive, depressed, dissatisfied, frustrated, lonely, reserved, responsible, and vulnerable. There were only two traits in common: conscientious and responsible. Those eight other traits for the least successful describe, in a way, the personality of a potentially suicidal person.

Negative indicators   The presence of certain negative indicators at a fairly early age (say before 20) seemed related to subsequent suicide in this group. These included alcoholism, suicide threats, homosexuality, conspicuous achievement failures, depression, neurasthenia (nervous exhaustion characterized by abnormal fatigability), marriage and divorce, and dyspnea (difficulty in breathing, e.g., asthma, emphysema). Here is an example of one individual. At age 7 his mother wrote: "He is inclined to take the line of least resistance." At the same time, his teacher rated him high in desire to excel, general intelligence and originality; and low in willpower, *optimism*, and truthfulness. She indicated that although he came from "a good home," he was inclined to be moody and sulky. At age 8 his mother said he was strong-willed and liked to have his own way, that school was easy, and that he was making excellent grades. At 10 his parents divorced. At age 12 his teacher reported that he was not a very good student and was doing only fair work and had lazy mental habits. At age 16 he graduated from high school with a C average. He did not attend college. In his twenties he became an artist. He married. After service in World War II he was unemployed and was described by his wife as "immature, unstable, irresponsible and extravagant." Because of his many affairs, his wife, although stating she was fond of him, left him. She called him impulsive, romantic, and unstable. In his thirties he worked for a while as a commercial artist. He wrote to Professor Terman, "I am the lemon in your group." His life, as indicated by his income as one criterion, was a series of ups and downs. He was dead at 55.

The vital role of the spouse   My reading of these cases led me to the belief that the behavior of one's spouse could be the difference between life and death. In the 30 cases I studied, it seemed that a wife who was hostile, nonsupporting, and actively competitive could indirectly play a role in her spouse's suicidal outcome. (I believe that this is equally true for deficient husbands and their possibly suicide-prone wives.) I remember especially one case in which the husband was the Terman subject, and wrote to Professor Terman almost regularly. He then married a loquacious, self-absorbed, highly competitive, bright young woman. She took over the correspondence and wrote long letters to Terman about the details of *her* proposed dissertation (at another university).

Her husband seemed to disappear from the records—she seemed to have swallowed him up. I said to myself, "Oh, oh. He's in trouble," and I put him among the five suicidal cases, and so he was. (Of course, there were many other indications.)

At a somewhat deeper level, and thus more theoretical, in the lives of these suicides there were: elements of childhood or adolescent rejection, disparity between aspiration and accomplishment, early (preadolescent) instability. At a still deeper level (and even more speculative) is the notion that the bright suicidal person is one who believes that he has not had his father's love and seeks it symbolically without success throughout his life, eventually hoping magically to gain it and escape the pain of rejection by a singular act of expiation. Those gifted men who committed suicide did not have that internalized approving parental homunculus that—like a strong heart—seems necessary for a long life. Melita Oden wrote that the "magic combination" for success in life among the gifted was not a simple one. I would add that for suicide the equation is also a combination of obvious and subtle elements. Many factors, none of which alone seems sufficient—although the corrosive effect of unbearable psychological pain comes the closest—coexist in a suicidal case where the negative, death-promoting elements overcome the normal, ordinary, almost ubiquitous life-sustaining habits of our days.

Up to this point, we have been talking about Terman Study men. Here is a woman—Natalie, who committed suicide by barbiturate overdose at age 40. In this case, I did not estimate "blindly" from a truncated record; instead, I knew that she had committed suicide before I looked at her file. Let me relate this sad case chronologically, as the records disclosed it.

The conditions of her birth were noted as "absolutely normal." She was breast fed until she was four months old. As an infant, she slept soundly.

At the age of five and a half she was given dancing lessons. There is a note that she was very enthusiastic and showed decided ability. When she was six, her mother wrote to a friend that "Edgar Guest's poems are her great favorites." In the same letter, her mother wrote: "I have tried to use a lot of common sense and answered every question to the best of my ability because she is an understanding child and will listen to reason. I have not had to stimulate a desire to learn because she always wanted to know everything her older playmates knew and she would try to learn voluntarily."

When Natalie was six years old, in the first grade, she was given the Stanford-Binet Intelligence Test. One item that she missed—although she scored exceptionally high overall with an IQ of 153, which put her in the extremely superior category—was this one: "Yesterday the police found the body of a girl cut into 18 pieces. They believed that she killed herself. What is foolish about that?" Her nonprophetic answer was: "She wouldn't kill herself." The psychologist noted, however, her general alertness and bright mind.

However, a very important event occurred in Natalie's life when she was seven: her father deserted her mother. Later in her life (at age 35), she noted, with obvious sadness, "My father never came to see me except once."

There is a record of her childhood medical examination, written by a school physician when she was eight, stating that she was "somewhat nervous, bordering on irritability." A school record at 11 notes that her last name had been changed to reflect the fact that her mother had divorced and remarried. Her teacher's report states that she was a "young-ster with an understanding and reasoning mind that at times surprises her family" and that "her courtesy and tact are remarkable."

At age 12, several items are noted in the record. She suffered from numerous headaches and had glasses prescribed. She experienced her menarche. She was a straight A student (in the seventh grade) and indicated that she wanted to go to college and would also like to be a dancer. Her main teacher reported that, although she was extremely bright, she "shrinks from opportunities for leadership." At about this time, she wrote that her new stepfather was devoted and kind to her.

She finished high school and went on to college, but did not graduate. At college she developed a close, lasting student-teacher relationship with Professor Terman; she wrote detailed letters to him for years. At the age of 25, having, in her own words, been "an unsuccessful secretary," her "ultimate goal" was to "be a successful homemaker." (Remember, this was the 1930s.) She married and almost immediately became pregnant. In the following two years, she and her husband lived in five different cities. "It is hard to develop interests in any one place," she wrote.

There is a gap in the record for five years. At age 30 she had two children and reports in a letter a "great tendency to worry and to extreme nervousness." Her husband was drinking rather heavily. There was a dramatic change in her own physical and psychological state. She wrote that she was "too tired even to wash the windows." She also reported a sharp pain in her side, and that her doctor had told her it was due to "neurotic tendencies." She wrote that she was "chronically worn out and tired and very unhappy in the marriage."

There is a painful letter to Professor Terman, written when she was 35:

Until I was 25 I didn't know there were such things as problems in this world, but since then with the exception of my two lovely children and my perfect relationship with my mother, I've had just one struggle after another, made one blunder after another. My husband and I bicker constantly. I've wanted to divorce him a thousand times and still I know that it is not the solution. We were both raised in broken homes and we both love our children too much. He comes home drunk at night far too often. He can't afford it. He refuses to look at the bills and says, "Why haven't you saved money?" I have no one to talk to. I feel like I'm cornered. My mother's youngest brother and my nearest neighbor both committed suicide in one month about a year ago.

In this same letter she said about her father: "I adored my father from afar. Our occasional meetings were unsatisfactory. My father is a very brilliant man—however, *he has little use for me*. He lives 20 minutes away but has been in our house only once for a few minutes in the past two years."

In another letter the following year she wrote of her children:

Our little ones are nice but the eldest still bites her fingernails and fights constantly with her younger sibling. She is the result of my selfishness. . . . Well I've poured out my heart and I'm a little ashamed. In my heart I never doubted that I could be a happy, relaxed, useful human being, but it's taking such a long time to get there.

Three years later, when Natalie was 39, she separated from her husband because of—indicated in another letter—"his violent temper, his selfishness and his drinking." Nine months later, she was divorced. Four months after the divorce was final (and he had already remarried) she was dead by suicide. She had struggled all her life with her need to be accepted by her father.

She left three suicide notes.

To her ex-father-in-law: Papa—no one could have been more kind or generous than you have been to me—I know you couldn't understand this—and forgive me—Mr. Dorcus has a copy of my will—Everything equal—the few personal things I have of value—the bracelet, my wedding ring, Nana's diamond—please have someone come in and clean— Have Bob take the children away immediately—I don't want them to stay around—You're so good Papa dear.

To her ex-husband: Bob—I'm making all kinds of mistakes with our girls—They have to have a leader and every day the job seems more enormous—They do love you— Nancy misses you so and she doesn't know what's the matter—I know you've built a whole new life for yourself but make room for the girls and keep them with you—Take them where you go—It's only for just a few years—Betty is almost ready to stand on her own two feet—But Nancy needs you desperately. Nancy needs help. She really thinks you don't love her, but she's got to be made to do her own part for her own self-respect—Nancy hasn't been hurt much yet—but ah! the future if they keep on the way I've been going lately—Barbara sounds warm and friendly and relaxed and I pray to God that she will understand just a little and be good to my girls—They need two happy people, not a sick, mixed-up mother—There will be a little money to help with the extras—It had better go that way than for more pills and more doctor bills—I wish to God it had been different but be happy, but please, stay by our girls—And just one thing—be kind to your Papa—He's done everything he could to help me—He loves the girls dearly and it's right that they should see him often—Natalie

To her two children: My dearest ones—You two have been the most wonderful things in my life—Try to forgive me for what I've done—Your father would be so much better for you. It will be harder for you for awhile—but so much easier in the long run—I'm getting you all mixed up—Respect and love are almost the same—Remember that—and the most important thing is to respect yourself—The only way you can do that is by doing your share and learning to stand on your own two feet—Betty, try to remember the happy times and be good to Nancy. Promise me you will look after your sister's welfare—I love you very much—but I can't face what the future will bring.

Her note to her ex-husband is a painful *mea culpa*. She takes the blame and pleads with him—a man who drank and was barely possible to live with—to be good to their children and she asks that the new stepmother and her ex-husband provide a stable, loving home for her girls. There was no note to her parents, both of whom lived—separately, of course—nearby.

Natalie's suicide note to her children is filled with contradictions and inconsistencies. The implicit logical arguments flow back and forth, between assertion and counterassertion, never with any resolution. She says, in effect, you will stay with your father, you should love your father, I know that you cannot love your father, but you should respect him. She then free-associates to the word "respect" and argues, rather lamely, that love and respect are almost the same anyway, and, in case that argument is not persuasive (which it is not), that one should at least respect oneself. The logic wanders. She then says to her children that they must stand on their own two feet, but also implies that the point of her removing herself from their lives is so that they can be reunited with their father—as probably she yearned to be reunited with *her* father.

What deep psychological strands of mental pain motivate such an act? When we read about her life, especially the subtleties of interaction with her father, we can see the malignant beginnings of her self-abnegating attitudes. At the end, she is so frantic, in so much pain, that she will give anything, make any votive offering, including her life, to achieve the feeling of lost childhood love.

In her suicide she reenacted her own earlier life drama—the yearning for her parents to be together and love her—and in this misdirected symbolic sacrifice, instead of giving her children a united home, she, in the most traumatic way possible, deprived them of their own mother. Her aspirations—to be her father's favorite, to care for and be cared for, to be symbolically reunited with her children in a happy home—were no better realized in her death than in her life.

I believe that important changes in the childhood-formed personality *can* occur in adolescence and adulthood, perhaps without limit as to age. Paradoxically, our experiences with people from two vastly different sources—returnees from extended stays in a war zone where the entire environment was psychotic, and unhappy patients in psychotherapy where only their homes were unsafe—teach us that salutary changes are possible, especially with psychotherapy—though not in all cases.

6

The Need to Belong:
The Case of Castro Reyes

Castro Reyes—born in the United States of Caribbean parents—shot himself in an unusual way. Somehow he obtained a MAC (Military Armament Corporation) .45 fully
automatic pistol, loaded with jacketed hollow-point bullets.
It is hard to picture exactly what he did—and I never
thought to question him about these details (which did not
seem pressing when I was seeing him subsequently). He
must have placed the gun to the right side of his face and
squeezed the trigger. Two rounds were instantaneously fired.
The bullets tore through his face, blew away many of his
teeth, most of his tongue, parts of his nose and cheekbone,
and destroyed his right eye. It was all over in a nanosecond.

His face was a bloodly mess, but his buzzing brain was untouched except for the irreparable memories of new kinds of pain.

The idiosyncrasy of his shooting reflected the strangeness of his person. There he was, in a small town in the southwestern United States, with an unusually bright mind (God's gift), unable to speak Spanish, precociously well-read and self-taught, a genuine autodidact, a serious student of, among many things, the Roman Caesars. Add to this a disturbed mother, no father at all, and no one to talk to—intellectually isolated and socially disaffiliated. Handsome and robust, with a penchant for cutting corners and defying the establishment. And with an active reputation for bisexuality in a community (and at a time) when that was taboo.

In the medical center where I worked (as a professor of thanatology) I was called to see him—about a week after the shooting. The young doctor said, "This patient is a pain in the ass." I was led to believe from that telephone conversation that the patient, "a young Latino male," was probably schizophrenic and maybe mentally retarded. The implied goal was to try to make him more tractable. He had made some motions as if to strike a nurse who was giving him a shot. At the time, his face was entirely bandaged and he was in his own total darkness.

I went up to the ward, to his bed, cleared my throat, and told him I had come to help him. I had brought a pad of paper and some ballpoint pens. Could we have an exchange? And so we started. In a few weeks, the bandages were taken off his left eye and he could see well enough to write on the pad. One sentence was enough to show me that he had an extraordinary command of the language (in spelling and grammar) and a somewhat stilted, almost high-flown, grandiloquent style. And an amazing vocabulary. This was no feebleminded fellow. And while he was obviously perturbed and had deep psychological problems, he was not acutely schizophrenic—although one could entertain the idea of what we professionals call over-ideational pre-schizophrenia. An immediate indication of his nonpsychotic status was his ready capacity to form a relationship with me, in which the patient trusts the therapist. We set a daily appointment time and I am not embarrassed to say that we both looked forward to that hour.

At the very beginning, "personal" topics seemed to be off limits, so I decided to interact with him—I talked; he wrote—about one of the special areas of his esoteric interests, the ancient Roman emperors. I read up on Caesar Augustus, Caligula, Nero, and the others. And if you had dropped in on one of those early sessions you might have thought either that we were having a college tutorial in ancient history, or that the therapist was out of his mind. But it was the coin of exchange between us. In his mind, he was talking to a therapist who amazingly knew something about *his* topic, Roman history. And, in my mind, I was feeding into his need for affiliation, the frustration of which had driven him to the most extreme measures.

Castro was not exactly an orphan; he was more like a displaced person. He was an involuntary "isolato"[1]; there was almost no one in his home community for him to talk to. He had secrets he could not discuss. Mostly, he was looking for friends. He had a burning need to affiliate with others, to make friends.

This chapter is an epistolary record. It consists almost entirely of his writings—over 200 separate items, either notes (written in his hospital bed) or letters (written from his home), addressed to me. The damage to his teeth and tongue and the loss of his lower jaw made his speech almost unintelligible. But could he ever write!

The Incident

Within some weeks of the shooting, Castro wrote an account of what went on in those terrible moments afterward—see Figure 1. Subsequently I asked Castro to write a more detailed recounting of the events preceding what he and I now referred to as "the incident." He responded with a 16-page account, from which the following is quoted.

I quit my job unable to work. This left me about to be evicted if I did not find another person quickly. I could find no one to share my place. Nor could I convince Marion [his boyfriend] to stay. I lost my appetite. In these times I slept a few hours at night. I worked [at a restaurant] long hours. Only to come home to another person who had another battle to throw at me....I went to my private altar. But there was no peace to be found. I thought what shall I do? I had done all I could and was still sinking. I sat there many hours seeking answers and all there was was a silent wind and no answers. I remember my words, "Are these the days of the end? What be the answer?" I heard "Wait." When I left the answer was in my head.

It was all clear now. Die. The next day my neighbor offered to sell me a gun. I bought it. My first thought was what a mess this is going to make. This day I began to say goodbye to people. Not actually saying it but expressing it silently. I went to church Sunday. I was at a loss of what to do. I did say goodbye to my sister that Sunday but I did not return to her house. Fasting began this day. I didn't sleep. Marion was still there yelling in my ear but I had since cut off his voice in my mind. One by one I turned off my outside channels to the world. Radio music was a blur of distorted melodies. The party for two I had planned was now designed and I got all my ingredients for it. For as much as I and Marion argued I still could call him friend. And

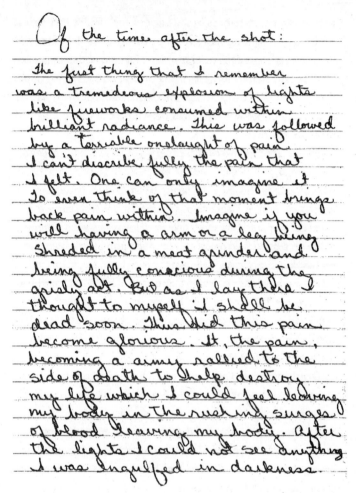

Of the times after the shot:

The first thing that I remember was a tremendous explosion of lights like fireworks consumed within brilliant radiance. This was followed by a terrible onslaught of pain. I can't discribe fully the pain that I felt. One can only imagine it. To even think of that moment brings back pain within. Imagine if you will having a arm or a leg being shreded in a meat grinder and being fully conscious during the grisly act. But as I lay there I thought to myself I shall be dead soon. Thus did this pain become glorious. It, the pain, becoming a army rallied to the side of death to help destroy my life which I could feel leaving my body in the rushing surges of blood leaving my body. After the lights I could not see anything I was engulfed in darkness.

Figure 1   A sample page of Castro Reye's writing.

so I would remain. But I made it a night he should remember ever through his life to the end of his days.

These last days become mixed to me. My mind became locked on my target. Even when I was asked out to have a good time I was not there. My thoughts were: Soon it shall be all over. I remember words in the back of my mind which struck home. I shall fight no more forever. By my death I would have life within the last dreams of my mind. I would obtain the peace I had sought so long for. This being the last threads of my hope. I did know I didn't wish to see the days ahead. For many battles had I fought. The war that I had been a part of for so long had taken its toll on me.

I could not find myself surrendering to all which I had feared. The armies of my fears had me encircled. I saw not nor had a plan of escape this time. My army of life and its resources. Its legions of money. Captains of schemes and will to survive and succeed. Had been crushed, defeated. I was like unto a general alone on a battlefield being encroached upon by my enemy and its hordes. Fear, hate, self-destruction. Demons in my mind telling me how easy it was to surrender. But always I felt I had to have the upper hand. To control my environment. Alone was I and I sought to die rather than surrender. Retain the last shard of my honor left. Never would I surrender. I would commit Seppuku. I had lost the war at last.

Death swallowed me long before I pulled the trigger. I was locked within myself, set on the final blow. The world through my eyes seemed to die with me. It was like I was to push the final button to end this world. I felt so weak, mentally wartorn, unable to fight anymore. There comes a time when all things cease to shine, when the rays of hope are lost. I committed myself to the arms of Death.

We have no trouble recognizing the tell-tale signs that we have seen before: psychological pain, frustrated needs, constriction, isolation, confused logic, and profound hopelessness.

Early on in his hospital stay, he wrote these notes: "I went outside the other night for about an hour. Outside by myself in my gown, out on the stairwell. It was a very cool night.

The moon was out amidst the clouds. A gentle breeze was blowing and I relaxed and sat upon the steps watching the stars for hours. There is a great peace in watching the night-time sky. A chance for undisturbed meditation. It reminds one of things such as how small man is in comparison to the universe being how big it is."

Reading these last lines brings to mind of one of the most unusual suicide notes I have ever seen. It is carved in a cypress tree near a spectacular waterfall, the Kegon Falls at Lake Chuzenji in Japan. That site and that note are known to many Japanese schoolchildren. The note was carved by Misao Fujimura, who committed suicide by throwing himself over the falls at age 25—the same age at which Castro shot himself—almost a century ago, in 1903. Some friends translated the note for me:

> Feelings at the top of the cliff, Kegon Falls: The world is too wide and history is too long to be evaluated by such a tiny thing as a five-foot creature. . . . The true nature of all being is beyond understanding. I have made up my mind to die with this problem. . . . Now at the top of the cliff I feel no anxiety.

There is more communion with nature in Misao's note and more concern with self in Castro's note. Nevertheless, the comparison between the miniscule size of a person's neurosis and the magnitude of the Milky Way is a universally humbling experience for any stargazer, East or West. In my mind, it speaks to the universality and ubiquity of psychological pain.

The Family

To paraphrase the opening line in Tolstoy's *Anna Karenina*: "Every happy family seems the same; every dysfunctional

family functions in its own unhappy way." Castro's family
consisted of a mother, a father who disappeared and a stepfather likewise, an older sister whom he adored, and a
younger brother whom he passionately hated. "My ancestry,"
he wrote, "stems from Italy, Spain, the Pyrenees, Scotch-
Irish, to the Apache Indian tribe, and some Caribbean buc-
caneers. A bit of everything. I would think of it as mostly
Roman-Indian." He had thick black hair, dark eyebrows, and
an overall swarthy look.

From a letter:

I really like your style of talking to me. You are frank and
to the point but you don't yell or say unnecessary things to
hurt. I only wish I had that kind of talking as I grew up. I
think I would be a different sort of person. As I grew up I
was scared of my mother. Afraid she would hit me. She never
talked to me. She yelled. What moral teaching and educational
learning I have I have done on my own. . . . But in spite of what
I had to work with I think I have had some success in my upbringing. I have something which I would like to bring up. I want
to know if it has any weight to it. I hate my younger brother
not just like other people would say but I actually hate him.
There is no love at all. If he were to die I would rejoice at his
death. He has not only stolen from me things of great value
but he has seen to it that my mother was mad at me most of
the time. In short he has done a lot of mischief in my life. I
have tried to like him but there is nothing to like. I loath his
very self.

In another:

Of the beginning days when I was a youth before I got bored
with what I had. I really don't ever remember being happy for
a prolonged time. . . . When I started school I didn't know

anyone. My mother didn't allow me or my sister to associate with what she called "gutter rats." Sure, my sister and I had our private playground, but both my sister and I were very lonely. . . . I remember the most famous of my mother's answers: "You think yourself common like those kids. You have everything here. Nothing but trouble is out there." . . . My sister and I, since we had only each other we played always together never fighting. My sister has always been close to me. We were often taken as twins. . . . At age 5, Felix, my new father, moved in with us. A man who tried to fill the position vacated by my father two years earlier. I only wish I had asked him how to make friends at school. At school I was a quiet boy, never really had any friends, I played with the girls. What I was accustomed to at home. Yet ever did I have the yearning to be like the other boys. My assets became that which I was not seeking. The little girls liked me. I talked to them and didn't fight with them. I acquired a habit. I liked to touch people. When I did meet people I would flood them with words trying to form some relationships and belong. I did not know all the customs of what not to do to other people, like touching. I truly wanted to experience what I could understand for lack of contact. . . . About this time Felix was hired to tend orchards for a man whose ranch was quite big and quite remote. We were deeply secluded now because our nearest neighbor was a mile away. But we had 100 acres of land to tend. This was a wilderness. To look out of my bedroom window as far as I could see was the land of the owner. . . . At age seven the worst of all of my days came to life when my half-brother was born. I can honestly say that I hated him from the first day. To this day I feel the same hate and the feeling that I should have killed him years ago. The school I went to was very small. We each had booths isolated from the others. It was here I learned many things by myself and my true home was that of Nature. Our actual

home was on a mesa. To the east were mountains and ter-
races, and below us was the woods. Often did Felix and I go
hunting. He taught me how to shoot. My grandfather also
talked to me. But he's dead now. He made the ring that I
wear now. He was the one I looked up to.... It was like being in a year-round summer camp. But I had no one to show
all my lands and streams. My work at that age was easy
enough. To walk around with my dogs and see if any fences
had been broken. Later I also learned to drive a tractor and
also the truck as well. This time of my life was indeed happy.
I liked having all that was around me. A boyhood dream. I
had the largest front yard of anyone I ever knew. Mountains
for a front yard and a valley for a backyard, complete with
forests and rivers. And in a sense it was ours. Felix's contract
was for life as long as the crops were produced and tended
and always available for the owner's needs. Thus we dwelt in
peace of solitude, our family, our animals, our home. Even
the stars felt like they were mine. I felt secure and worried
not about tomorrow back then. Yet the dark clouds of
change found us at last one day. I shall not forget that day.
We all awoke to mom. She was looking for Felix. He was
gone. We searched for days. We never found him. He simply
left. The changes that followed afterward became degrading
and even worse. We could not stay on the land and had to
move. Another school again and still no friends. Socially we
slid down the scale. My mother found us a place to live but it
was worse than I had ever known. My dear sister was sent to
live with my grandmother. To this point in my life "poor"
was associated with other people. The very thought sickened
me for by now it had developed in my mind that other people were of the common folk. How could we associate with
them? All my life thus far I had been shielded from the pop-
ulace and now to be a part of it disgusted me at first. Even at
school I didn't go to a regular school. There was isolation

and study groups. And so what we learned was what they were teaching in high school. But home never was like this before. We had become part of the masses.... During this time I grew very interested in history and ancient cultures. Maps depicting history. My aspiration at that time was to be become a teacher of history, military history. I would pick a book on European history and wars, immerse myself in facts and ideologies of great people. Study Caesar, Charlemagne, Napoleon. The great rebirth of cultures. I would gladly have given reports to the class, but my speech would never allow this to become possible. During this time I had a stuttering problem. Sometimes it got so bad I could not complete a short sentence. But it was my social attitude that the school officials didn't like. The wars of the playground always were at the attention of the faculty. But in the playground a new 'nation,' mine, had sprung up and like all bullies we began to push out the weaker ones.

Back in the hospital, Castro wrote me a note about his mother and the topic of "touching."

As my memory serves me there was a time when I did not have a problem with people touching me. Truly it has caused great problems between my mother and me. Since childhood I have found that I can't stand to have anyone touch my person. It is as if I am being violated. Surely with my mother this should not be so. Yet many times she has tried to hug me or come close to me and show the affection that already been sorely lacking. It is a feeling that I can't seem to control. And when those times of affection do occur I feel great regret because I can see the hurt in my mother's face and the tears that flow. Then after seeing her hurt so I really hate myself because I can't control myself from shunning her so. When in fact I long for her to hug me and let her feel the love I have for her. I hate even more the fact that those moments are lost in the past. Yet with other people I do not feel regret. I feel that if I don't give them permission then it is a violation. Memories of when I first started in school reveal it was I who was the toucher. In fact it was part of my communication. I felt I had to touch a person. The reasons for this act remain a mystery. But in school because I would touch mostly girls with long braids of hair or pretty dresses. These acts were always followed by a chastising from the teachers. They never told me why I was acting wrong, they just said it was wrong. After chewing me out, the yelling was closely followed by strict punishment. Time after time I would find myself at the receiving end of the principal's paddle. Which is to say it was beat into me that touching others was wrong. Mind that this conviction was not realized in my conscious mind but rather my subconscious mind. Logically applying that if it was wrong to touch others then the same could be true about others touching me. But this application did not leave any space for those reaching out to me in love. Greatest of all, my mother. Yet because I never addressed the "problem" it was left to fester like a wound untended spanning the years getting worse and the reasons for being so may not be only this one in school. Perhaps it lies deeper and further back in the past, locked away in forgetfulness. But since the incident I did address this situation and began changing it gradually now in the days of peace between my mother and me. I have applied these changes to our relationship. It truly has been an instrumental part in sealing the wounds of hurt that the years had laden us with. Lying here in the hospital bed I find peace in the knowledge that all at home is well and that she loves me. But best of all is that she knows that I love her....I have written my mother again. I hope she will answer me this time. I miss her very much. It hurts within me. I feel cut off from my family. I must pause for today, like Shakespeare wrote, "My heart lieth there with Caesar. I must pause til it come back to me."

Sex, Love, and Drugs

Age 13 Met Victoria Olocci, friend, introduction of Marijuana. The girl likes me, however, it stays at agape stage.

Age 14 Summer spent isolated preparing for next school year. More accumulation of Knowledge. My sister introduces Dolores, my first girlfriend. Sexual contact achieved.... The high mark of this year was a beautiful new teacher Miss Gleiss age 28. Becomes my date for graduation at my request. This event started rumors of sexual events which never happened and destroyed a purely friendly relationship.

Age 16 *Star Wars* comes out. Through the summer I see it 57 times.... My niece Beverly Ann is born. I am proud of my sister. She is a jewel in my heart... While in history class I am caught sleeping. As a punitive action the teacher tells me to teach the class on the time of the French Revolution to Napoleon. To his surprise I accomplished this easily and in more detail than he. Afterward I told him that Napoleon was one of my favorite subjects. I was never bothered again.... My drug use [of cocaine] increases to at least two ounces a week.

Age 17 The trip to the city went well, to have him ship me a certain amount of pot at city price and sell at my price which was almost double. I accomplished my task and made a considerable high profit deal.... My car was a used police car still equipped with whatever makes them go so fast. I used to like the thrill of doing 115 mph on the highway coming back from long runs out of town. When I didn't want to pull over for the police all I had to do is turn off the headlights and do 70 mph fast. Spending as much as $100 a night on cocaine, partying and entertainment.... It was on my birthday Luella came over to my place and on this day did we finally make Love not Sex. But Love. I guess she got what she wanted but I asked her to leave me be for three days that I might consider the feelings in my heart to their truest aspects. I went to my private altar where I stayed and fasted for three days. And so it was to be. When I returned to Luella I had found my love for her was indeed Love and not lust. We grew even more the closer.

Age 18 This birthday is best remembered by me for its extravagance. I began my party on a Friday and ended on Monday. I bought 7 kegs of my favorite beer. I bought enough cocaine and pot to get the whole party thoroughly stoned. It was by invitation only but as it progressed this plan was futile. I bought 2 pounds of pot which was dumped on the table to partake at leisure. I got a lot of presents of drugs including six doses of LSD. Through the party I got laid by 5 girls, two being virgins. Birthday presents. It almost became an orgy.

A note added in the present What I see looking in a mirror of the mind: A maverick, for I strive to be unlike my peers. Not by any means humble. I am self-centered. I adore perfection. I love history and would if I could become part of those old days. I hate ignorance and people who lack common sense. I like beautiful blond women. I love art, not confining my love to a canvas or stone but to music, literature, the arts of one's mind even if it displays itself. I would explore the unknowns of time if I could choose the course to sail. I like soft delicate things like that of the rose. I don't really like money itself but I do like what it can buy. I like my nests of fantasy that I might escape to in a moment's notice. I have a dual character and appearance. I have my armor that protects me and projects a mask that lets the outside see what I wish it to see. I love things that over-stimulate me. Within me is a world all unto itself. A universe where I am king and master. And yet there are regions within that are against me. The evil ones, my enemies. From whence my wars come. At times I am eager to war. And times of peace and contentment. I seek thrills not caring about the after-effects. But rather to feel the experience of the thrill. I would love to stride among the stars and create my own reality. I would like to ascend to the heavens and walk with God. I would like to stop time and turn back disaster. I would like to compose music. And watch as the notes go flying off in the air. I would like to leave my mark in history. . . . I love children. They bring out protective qualities in me. This protective feeling is not limited to children. I inflict it upon everyone I know. Sometimes caring too much. I care more for love rather than sex. I lust for love but I don't love for lust. For I am yet I am not. For I am yet unfinished even as I close my eyes only for a moment and that moment is gone. Just a drop of water in an endless sea.

In her pioneer work on male homosexuality, Evelyn Hooker, UCLA professor emerita—now almost in her nineties—discovered that there were about as many maladjusted heterosexuals as homosexuals, and about as many well-adjusted homosexuals as heterosexuals. Castro Reyes was unhappy in his sexuality, or, perhaps more accurately, he was a bisexual person who was unhappy in his close relationships.

I hasten to add that I have no worthwhile theory as to the etiology of adult sexual orientation; whether one should best study genetic disposition, hormones, early psychological experiences, the presence or absence of male or female role models, or what have you. It is not a field about which I can speak with any authority. In my view, homosexuality relates to suicide as psychological pain relates to suicide. If it doesn't hurt, it doesn't count.

Castro wrote several letters and notes on this general topic, in detail about the social intricacies and difficulties with this or that intimate friend.

Here, from among many, are three letters or bed-written notes that touch on this theme.

I am composed again. I looked out of my window today it is raining. I love the rain. I think of the drops on my window the sound of rain. All are beautiful to my senses.... Two more days til surgery again. I want to make a step forward. I thought of two more books I would like to hear. *Moby-Dick* and *The Count of Monte Cristo*. The two books I have chosen could be called obsession and revenge. I feel adventurous.... I remember more things to add to my list. When I first awoke in intensive care in the hospital near my home I thought to myself, It didn't work. I can't even kill myself right. I felt broken both in heart and in spirit. I also thought where was Jim. Did he hate me now. He knew before all this that I was sick. He had a hand in my self-destruction. Tearing up my last defenses. I needed someone to stand by me then. But he too attacked me like all the rest. We were at war. Though in the end I didn't fight back. In fact, my last wish was to leave friends. I had my last party with him alone. I was determined to leave friends. I even left him a note saying, "Even in the end I did call you friend forever will you be to me." I should hope that those words burned in his mind forever.... I would hope that those people whose lives I have touched will remember me and what I gave to them. A part of me in some way.

It seemed as though suicide and homosexuality were subjects he could not leave. Another letter, two years after the previous one:

Herein lies deep roots into why things happened as they did. Fragments of sorrow, despair, depression and of course love. They are linked to one element which is named Jim. Not just the person but the very concept. I shall begin as all things should at the beginning when I first met Jim, the first of many Jims. Until I met this young boy of 13, I had never known real love in my life. I had girlfriends before but they never stirred my heart. Before I met him my heart was barren longing for someone who loved me like I wanted. I had never before considered myself desirable to others. But for the first time I had a very cute guy who loved me. I could believe that for once I was happy. It was a situation that I surely didn't want to end. He was really my first love. Even as I look back now I suppose I still love him. But like so many things since it was not mine for long.

A person who claimed to be my friend decided to put his interests before our friendship. While I was in the hospital he literally stole my boyfriend from me. I didn't know until later but it happened. This is the first time I couldn't control the situation. I had no cure for what happened. Even telling him what this was doing to me couldn't help. Deep depression set in. I had no solution. My love was ripped from me. This was the time I first tried to commit suicide. I didn't want to see what was happening right before my eyes. But that first attempt failed. I then decided to try to win back Jim but failed. But other aspects of my life which I had neglected now overcame me and I became lost in my job. I had become too busy to think about Jim. I thought of him daily as I still do but not all day. A few months later he contacted me. We went out again for a few weeks until William called him and he returned to him once more. I felt I was being used. Crying nightly before I slept became a common occurrence.

He may not have ever loved me but I surely loved him. That was all that really mattered. I opened my heart to him and he crushed it. To this day I have yet to open my heart so. I promised myself I would never let myself be hurt so again. If it could be measured I gave 100% of it. It hurts even now to think of him and what once was. Since that time a real love relationship has not touched my life. The next Jim in the picture was Jim Boxer. Though we were lovers we never committed to the love that was like Jim. It was that lacking that caused our eventual breakup. There became a mystique about the name Jim inside. When I hear or speak that name I get this strange feeling inside. Chills. A love song comes on the radio and I'll think of him. He began to become so sacred to me that I could not have any relationships at all. Then I met Jim. Once again the name was there. One more factor that I must relate is that each one of these Jims had blond hair and blue eyes.

"I found Jim Cook through Ford. He was and still is a very good friend. But to my gay friends Jim was referred to as my lover. He wasn't but I didn't deny it. It became so important to me to have a Jim in my life no matter what the status. I even began the fantasy that we really were lovers. I treated him as if he was. I told him about myself and the fantasy. He didn't care. We went out on dates and did everything lovers do except sex. I even upon occasion told him I loved him. But he was straight and as I said before we never had sex. I began to think that this situation was acceptable. The name Jim was there along with I love you. Jim Cook introduced me to Jim #4 whose last name was Taft. This Jim I did have sex with, but once more I was unable to love him the way he wanted. The degrees of love for each one of these Jim's was never 100% but I did find myself in love with each for his name's sake.

Fantasy began to win over reality with Jim #5. His name was Jim Ripley. He like Jim Cook was straight but this time I didn't tell him. I treated him as if he was my lover. In my fantasy world he was my lover. To my gay friends he was because I told them so. A Jim to say daily to myself I love you Jim. In conversation the words "Jim and I have a date tonight." But in each case I treated them so much like the real thing that the strain broke the friendship. Because them not knowing, they could not understand. Except for Jim Cook. It got to the point that I really did love him. But I couldn't have all of him which I began to want. But if I wanted to continue to have him as a friend this could never happen. He is now 21. I find him leaving for the Navy. Now I faced a new dilemma. No Jim.

But exactly two days later I met Jim Blythe, the last Jim. The one that I lived with at the time of the incident. My problem of having a Jim was solved. He too was straight but as before I treated him like he was a lover. To his knowledge I was just a good friend. Which I really was but the motivation was his name and appearance. The hair and eyes. It was also in these days I began to increase the amount of LSD in my life. One night under the influence I ran into Jim #1 while with Jim #6. He wanted to go out with me. But I couldn't let the other find out. So I met him later. I told him that he was my new Jim. Afterwards it became apparent to me that I still had the same feelings for him. I thought that time had taken that away but it was not so.

Are these the words of a man whose mind is clouded by drugs and liquor? Or is it an obsession? Is it an *idée fixe*? An over-ideational runaway in his mind? Castro never got these vital things—friendship, love, touching, what was right and wrong (the rules)—quite straightened out. He still wished that his stepfather, Felix, had taught him how to get along with his peers in elementary school.

But his sexual identity, while coming from mixed skeins in his body and mind, was clear toward the end. A woman made an advance toward him and he was morally outraged.

I neglected to mention a circumstance on June 18. I went to my sister's house for a little while. They were having a barbeque and others were there. Of them there was one girl who was a friend of my sister. She had been drinking and she started to become very friendly with me. This being a big surprise. I also thought that it must have been the drink.

But evidently it was not because this girl now tries to see me everyday. This is not to my liking and in fact I find it quite annoying. My eyes are for another and can't be swayed. Be it a test [of sexual orientation] or no, it makes me uneasy. Especially to have this girl advancing so. That is not her place. I don't like such forwardness.

Once I asked Castro about photographs of himself before the incident—I reasonably assumed there were some—and whether or not he might want to show them to the chief plastic surgeon. Oh, no, he said. He did not want his reconstructed face to have any resemblance to what he had looked like before. He wrote: "How many people get a chance to have two identities?" Two different lives in one lifetime? Previously, he had mentioned yin and yang. And he had written that he and his beloved sister—the closest companion of his life—had sometimes been mistaken for twins. Castro was a closet *Doppelganger*, whose twin would, somehow, be a pretty girl.

A Touch of Power

Within Castro's complicated personality there was a curious, manipulative, controlling, domineering streak, coming close to, but never quite bursting into, overt sadism. This thread seemed unconsciously connected with his hidden homosexuality. At times, it manifested itself in petty, behind-the-scenes ways of controlling other people's lives. Castro's pleasure seemed to come not only from the act of manipulating, but also from his private knowledge that the person being manipulated was not aware that he, Castro, was the true source of power. He liked being the king's lieutenant, the prime minister's Chief Whip, the mafia boss's enforcer. All of the clout; none of the responsibility.

In one of his letters he wrote about high school:

My school years are dear memories to me. When I was in school, I had a part in many things. . . . The President's Council was my most influential job. We made policy for our school. The School Board felt that we the students could best judge our peers. . . . Individual petitions were presented to the Senate, who voted on them and then sent them to the Council for ratification. There were four of us beside the president. I decided cases involving fighting, smoking on campus, cutting. The president voted only in case of tie. His job was a totally boring position. I much preferred "ruling from behind the throne," and I could get almost anything done in my favor within the Student law. . . . I found my job very easy to do. I could say to a Senator if I decide against your policy you will lose your bid for re-election. To the president of a club I could say that I can suspend some member. To a counselor I could say you pass mine and I'll pass your policy. I found myself in the most enviable position I could ever have in the whole student body.

A few weeks later he wrote:

Did you ever see the Acropolis? Polis means city. New York is a megalopolis. I have heard many myths about Delphi. I have studied much on Greece and Rome. . . . I actually did think about Pyrrhus and how he did win and lost much. I would rather be like Caesar. I like his style of I came, I saw, I conquered. I believe a conqueror should cut the head from the snake first and abruptly and then he may cut up the rest at his leisure. I do know when to be nice and omnipotent but I also know when to be arrogant and unruly. I should think I am more of the former than the latter.

The next day he wrote me:

There are many aspects of my doctrine but the goal is to be first and foremost paramount monarch of each particular sphere of my life. How I realize this depends solely upon the enemy. If I must commit 10 wrongs to achieve a goal I shall. Making sure of no drastic retaliation against me. I find that I run my life like a chess game. Divide and conquer, crush all who stand in my way. Spare no one. Manipulate friends against each other thus weeding out opposition to my rule. Though I may have many different circles of friends it is I who is unquestionably ruler. So it can be said that if a person become a liability to me, to that circle he shall die. Turning one against the other, weaving deceit between them. Exposing to all the weakness of the enemy. There may come a time of clemency but not until something gainful is apparent to me. Case in point: Oscar and William were friends. . . . And so in the end he offered more of himself than normal. I raked in the advantages. Taking complete control of him and his life. He of course yielded totally. So this case illustrates the unlimited boundaries of attack I am willing to exert. But now as I look back I think of Oscar's emotions and how I played with them. But then it didn't seem to matter. All I wanted was control of the prize.

Whatever hostilities Castro had boiling within him, he turned—as surely as if he had carefully studied the early Freudians—those feelings initially held toward others inwardly against himself. The early psychoanalysts had asserted that suicide was mainly unconscious hostility directed inward against the ambivalently viewed (loved-and-hated) internalized image of the father, sometimes transferred to the handsome and favored male sibling. Some years before I had called this view of suicide murder in the 180th degree, by which I meant that in some angry people suicide is the alternative to murder. This anger is also present, but in a more benign way, in Castro. This touch of anger constituted the darkest side of Castro and, I believe, was an integral part of his undoing.

The Barren Thread of Loneliness

Suffering is half pain and half being alone with that pain. For some people, suicide is feeling entirely alone. Castro's inner disputation was between his needs for autonomy, inviolacy, privacy, independence, on the one hand, and, on the other, his needs for friendship and affiliation. He could never seem to resolve them. Intellectually, he could distinguish among lust, love, sex, eros, agape, but in his boyish heart he never got over his need for companionship. The sticky point was that when he walked among the stars and spoke to God he didn't want anyone with him; in fact, he couldn't visualize a companion on those trips. But he was crushed by loneliness. He wrote to me about it over and over.

> Inside me it is as if I have been building a wall to protect myself. But from what? Like the wall that surrounds my house. I am building a wall of armor within. I guess it has been a life-time endeavor. And what people see of the inner me comes through the holes of decay or spaces yet to be filled. One day my sanctuary will be fully wrought but I have made no plans for a door, for a door invites invasion and violation of my inner peace. Yet once within my sealed wall what shall I become? For within I should prosper in my knowledge and wisdom. For surely once completed none can pass into my fortress of solitude. But, alas, all of these plans invite decay and loneliness. . . . Now there is a new war inside of me. One side says try again, and the other says remember what happens when you do. Wisdom says: The ox is slow but the earth is patient. I think the war shall end with

the finish of the walls of my citadel. When I shall stand on
the parapet and look out over the lands and seas of people
and ponder the decision to venture forth over new relations
or to protect me and my sanctuary forever. . . . I wonder how
long I will feel safe like this but for now there is peace in
my life. I hope you will write soon and communicate with
me. Until then I shall wait for your reply. . . . Help me. I
have no answers. I have no one else to turn to who under-
stands me, who knows what I've been through. Please re-
spond soon. I must regain control and find the solution.
R.S.V.P. . . . I now reach out to you for help. My mind is
sick. I need your kind words, your much learned advice.
Even if the help is not kindly it is still done in kindness. I
ask you, what sayest you to my plight. What guidance can
you give me in these most turbulent times. I feel as if I
stand at a crossroad, one leading to enlightenment and up-
wards, the other to an abyss and dark desolation of voided
emptiness of a closed mind both cut off from reality and
even myself. I ask you. Help me while time still exists to
help. Grant me guidance. Who else do I have to turn to?

I responded to this letter by telephoning him immedi-
ately. The crisis was about his current lover, and I did what
I could to deescalate the tension.
Then:

I must apologize for not writing you sooner than this but I
have had to spend a great deal of time getting my homelife
back in order. Truly it does seem to me that a void spans
between our last meeting and now. Since I have returned
home I have had a strange feeling of loneliness though circumstances have not changed in any way. It is as a new birth
in my feelings. Steady companionship is one so sorely
missed. I try so hard to cover over this yearning by being
busy. But it is at night that specters of passed loves come
calling to remind just how alone I really am. . . .

And a poignant note written when he was back in the hospital for an additional surgical procedure:

I hated torn roots. My friends, the ones I have and have had, have always been temporary ones. Lasting forever short of what I wished. When relations did cease I felt like I missed something. For I never really had a long-term friend. Those that did stay for a while the ongoing developments were always destructive to the relationship. I knew not the proper way of making things last. So did I always feel alone.

Even when I did have friends because of the shortcomings I never had any time for them. I needed time that I might develop and release my inner self and banish this loneliness. Even to the days of the incident it was so.

I do not fear many things in this life. Most of those were feelings rather than material. The fear of loneliness has been one of the strongest fears of my mind. Death to me is not a fear. Because it is definite and certain to come to all with the passing of years. I feel, in thought, that to fear death is too close to a "Living Death." But loneliness I could not bear, and I strive ever and again to defeat it. Yet the fear is that defeat will come surely to me, as destiny to the world. And so it is this thing or being that haunts me even now.

The Need for Affiliation and Friendship

The antidote to loneliness is friendship and affiliation. The most obvious alternative to being an "isolato" (whom even the Fates have no interest in kidnapping) is to love others (and to be vulnerable to their being kidnapped and your being held for emotional ransom). Alas, poor Castro. He knew no one well.

From the very beginning, my view of Castro was that he was motivated primarily by the affiliative need of friendship—and, secondarily, by his needs for dominance, inviolacy, sentience, and understanding. But mostly, through it all, by his need to be in congenial human company. Friendship is the single most frequent theme in his writings. He yearned for it. The frustration of this need was most powerful for him. He died for it.

As we know, the designer of this whole need-oriented psychology was Henry Murray. In his *Explorations in Personality*, he defined the need affiliation as "a positive tropism for people." In a way, it is the opposite side of narcissism, which is the need for affiliation turned inwards. It is not too difficult to see the towering narcissism in Castro—that hard, independent side—just as it is not difficult to see the soft, yearning side of his need for affiliation. Here is Murray:

> *Affiliation:* To draw near and enjoyably cooperate or reciprocate with an allied Other; to please and win affection of a cathected Other; to adhere and remain loyal to a friend; to have companions with similar interests; to affiliate and form friendships; to avoid wounding and to allay opposition; to converse in a friendly way, to give information, to tell stories, to exchange sentiments; to confide, to exchange secrets; to communicate, converse, telephone, write. The aim of the need for Affiliation is to form mutually enjoyable, enduring, harmoniously cooperating and reciprocating relationships with other persons, with a co-equal, a younger dependent, a pupil, a teacher.[2]

One can see that Castro's relationship to me was a projection, a transference, an acting out, a living through of his need to affiliate. Many of the letters he sent to me were begun with the word "Friend" and ended with "Your Friend." Some months after the incident he wrote "those days were filled with a turmoil that words cannot fully describe. They were truly filled with people screaming above the masses to me with one word that in dire need I wished to hear. FRIEND! Often these people held high that shield of honor displaying it proudly to me. But many times it was because they wished to hide their deceit and their own webs of self gain."

Castro reminded me of Edwin Arlington Robinson's poem "Minever Cheevy" and of De Rougemont's stimulating book, *Love in the Western World*—the interesting work about the medieval (and current) tradition of romantic and courtly love.[3] I viewed Castro as almost hopelessly in the romantic tradition—with the romantic's penchant for exaggerating and dramatizing fantasies, and imbuing his own fantasies with a certain hyperbolic and mythic quality. It rang out in the charming but slightly overheated quality of his prose, and in his obsessional pursuit of blond, blue-eyed men, all with the same talismanic name. I resisted (and do to this day) pegging him with a label. It was obvious, in plain English, that he had a severe personality disorder. He was not psychotic; he had a sort of Don Quixote, Minever Cheevy, Merlin the magician, troubadour—forever picking at his guitar—syndrome. What I am certain of is that he was enormously interesting, wonderfully appealing, and absolutely unique.

A Sad Postscript

There was a period of a few months during the fifth year in which we did not correspond. I took it for granted that he was all right (and that there is a time to leave patients alone) and that I would see him when he returned to the hospital for his next round of reconstructive surgery. Then one day I was shocked to my marrow to learn that he was dead; gunshot wound to the head—almost exactly five years after his first attempt. He had just turned 30.

Some weeks afterward, I received a letter from a mental health worker in his remote community. She wrote:

> He loved a young man named Harding more than anything and without him saw no reason to live. He needed peace more than life although he loved life too. He had a fixation with death and had toyed with the idea for the past several years. He said that someday he would finish the job he had started, and only he knew when. After he died it was discovered that Harding used to beat him. He had a lot of black and blue marks on him and he would say that he had fallen down. . . .

Castro had become thin and weak. He had no mouth or jaw and had not eaten any solid food for the five years since the shooting. (He existed on liquid Isocal, which he poured through a funnel into his gastric tube.) His biceps and pectoral muscles, which had been conspicuously robust, had become somewhat atrophied and desiccated. He was physically weak and emotionally exhausted, drained by physical pain. And worse: he was reliving the quarrel and rejection and loneliness of five years before. And this time his aim was deadly.

Between the two shootings, Castro underwent a number of operations, reparative plastic surgeries for bone grafts and skin grafts to construct a new jaw and reconstruct his face. I know that he endured days and nights of excruciating pain, in his hip and chest, from which bone, cartilage, and skin had been taken.

After he had returned home (following one of his several surgeries), he had written:

> The bravery that I must exert each day shows that I did have it in me to make it all work. I look upon what I could be and know that it could be done. These things all seem so simple compared with the hardships of now. I don't mean

times are hard. But that I wonder how many people in my place could go through what I have gone through and have yet to experience. . . . There is always relief upon returning home. I shall close for now and hope to hear from you soon. Until then I wish you Welcome back and Safe health. Your Friend.

One Veterans' Day I wore a miniature military ribbon in my lapel—an Army Commendation Medal from my service as a young captain in World War II. Castro saw it and admired it. Later that week I went to an Army surplus store and purchased one for him and then, the next day, at our meeting in his room, awarded it to him for having been a good soldier in the hospital.

Of course, many people, at the hospital and in the community, worked with Castro and tried to help him. These included a top team in reconstructive surgery, nurses, social workers, community agency workers, staff workers of government agencies and the Braille Institute, all sorts of good people. Except for the few rare times when he was (understandably) difficult, he was, even with his massive facial disfigurement, inexplicably charming and appealing, and, on some occasions, powerfully pathetic. Everyone who knew him was saddened by his death.

This chapter is dedicated to his memory.

PART FOUR

Staying Alive

7

Commonalities of Suicide

Like food for a starving person or new clothes for a liberated concentration camp prisoner, new ideas create new hope. This is true for both the suicidal person and the therapist. For me, the new idea was that all suicidal patients—that is, all the committed suicidal people I have studied over the years, independent of their different psychological needs—exhibited a certain set of psychological characteristics. In the cauldron of thought, I boiled these down to 10 commonalities of suicide.[1]

By "commonality," I mean a feature that is present in at least 95 out of 100 committed suicides—an aspect of thought, feeling, or behavior that occurs in almost every case of suicide. I am not talking about suicide among males, or suicide among African Americans, or suicide among teenagers, or suicide among manic-depressives. I am talking about *suicide*—all suicide. I wish to focus not so much on age, sex, ethnic status, or psychiatric diagnosis, but more on specific cases of suicide so that we can understand the personality of the suicidal person—and, of course, why they are driven to such an extreme act.

Here are the 10 psychological commonalities of suicide that I have found in my studies. (See Table 3.)

1. The common *purpose* of suicide is to seek a *solution*. Suicide is not a random act. It is never done without purpose. It is a way out of a problem, a dilemma, a bind, a difficulty, a crisis, an unbearable situation. For Ariel, Beatrice, or Castro—and everyone else—the idea of suicide acquired an inexorable logic, taking on an impetus of its own. Suicide becomes *the* answer—seemingly the only available answer to a real puzzler: How can I get out of this? What am I to do? The purpose of suicide is to solve a problem, to seek a solution to a problem generating intense suffering. To understand what a suicide is about, we must know the psychological problem the suicidal person intends to address. As Ariel told us, she needed to do something so that she "would hurt no more." Castro reiterated this purpose: "I would obtain the peace that I had sought so long for."

2. The common *goal* of suicide is *cessation* of consciousness. Suicide is best understood as moving toward the complete stopping of one's consciousness and unendurable pain, especially when cessation is seen by the suffering person as the solution—indeed the perfect solution—of life's painful and pressing problems. The moment that the possibility of stopping consciousness occurs to the anguished mind as *the* answer or *the* way out, then the igniting spark has been added and the active suicidal scenario has begun. "I com-

Table 3 Ten Commonalities of Suicide

- THE COMMON PURPOSE OF SUICIDE IS TO SEEK A SOLUTION.
- THE COMMON GOAL OF SUICIDE IS CESSATION OF CONSCIOUSNESS.
- THE COMMON STIMULUS OF SUICIDE IS UNBEARABLE PSYCHOLOGICAL PAIN.
- THE COMMON STRESSOR IN SUICIDE IS FRUSTRATED PSYCHOLOGICAL NEEDS.
- THE COMMON EMOTION IN SUICIDE IS HOPELESSNESS-HELPLESSNESS.
- THE COMMON COGNITIVE STATE IN SUICIDE IS AMBIVALENCE.
- THE COMMON PERCEPTUAL STATE IN SUICIDE IS CONSTRICTION.
- THE COMMON ACTION IN SUICIDE IS ESCAPE.
- THE COMMON INTERPERSONAL ACT IN SUICIDE IS COMMUNICATION OF INTENTION.
- THE COMMON PATTERN IN SUICIDE IS CONSISTENCY OF LIFELONG STYLES.

---

mitted myself to the arms of death"—this was Castro's way of telling us that he wanted all things to stop, now, permanently.

3. The common *stimulus* in suicide is psychological *pain.* If cessation is what the suicidal person is moving toward, psychological pain (or psychache) is what the person is seeking to escape. In any close analysis, suicide is best understood as a combined movement toward cessation and a movement away from intolerable emotion, unbearable pain, unacceptable anguish. No one commits suicide out of joy. The enemy to life is pain. "I died inside." "I was hurting very badly inside." "Overflowing waves of pain washed

though my body." Pain is the core of suicide. Suicide is an exclusively human response to extreme psychological pain, the pain of human suffering. I believe that if any one of us is able to capture the attention of a suicidal person, the key is to address the pain. If we are able to reduce the level of another person's suffering, even just a little bit, that individual may then see options other than suicide and can choose to live.

4. The common *stressor* in suicide is frustrated psychological *needs*. As we have seen in the cases of Ariel, Beatrice, and Castro, suicide stems from thwarted, blocked, or unfulfilled psychological needs. That is what causes the pain and pushes the suicidal act. To understand suicide in this context, we need to ask a much broader question: What is the psychological underpinning of most human acts? The best non-detailed answer is that, in general, human acts are intended to satisfy a variety of human *needs*. Of course, most suicides represent combinations of various needs. At a fundamental level, the suicidal person believes the act of suicide has a purpose. There are many pointless deaths, but every suicidal act reflects some specific unfulfilled psychological need.

5. The common *emotion* in suicide is *hopelessness-helplessness*. At the beginning of life, the infant experiences a number of emotions (rage, bliss) that quickly become differentiated. In the adolescent or adult suicidal state, the pervasive feeling is that of helplessness-hopelessness. "There is nothing I can do [except commit suicide], and there is no one who can help me [with the pain I am suffering.]" The early psychoanalytic formulations about suicide emphasized unconscious hostility, but today we suicidologists know that there are other deep basic emotions. The underlying one of these is that emotion of active, impotent ennui, the despondent feelings that everything is hopeless and I am helpless. Castro put it this way: "The rays of hope are lost."

6. The common *cognitive state* in suicide is *ambivalence*. Freud brought to our unforgettable attention the psychological truth that transcends the surface appearance of neatness of logic by asserting that something can be *both* A and not-A at the same time. We can both love and hate the same person. "I can't really say if I hate you or love you." Ariel told us: "It all came out that I really did love my father. I thought I hated him." We are of two minds about many important things in our lives. I believe that people who are actually committing suicide are ambivalent about life and death at the very moment they are committing it. They wish to die *and* they simultaneously wish to be rescued. As the young woman said about her walking across the steel beam at the hospital, "[I was] hoping that someone would see me out of all those windows; the whole building is made of glass." The prototypical suicidal state is one in which an individual cuts his throat and cries for help at the same time, and is genuine on both sides of the act. Ambivalence is the common state in suicide: To feel that one has to do it, and, simultaneously, to yearn for intervention. I have never known anyone who was 100 percent for wanting to commit suicide without any fantasies of possible rescue. Individuals would be happy not to do it, if they didn't "have to." It is this omnipresent ambivalence that gives us the moral imperative for clinical intervention. In a life-and-death struggle, why would any civilized person not throw in on the side of life?

7. The common *perceptual state* in suicide is *constriction*. I am one who believes that suicide is not best understood as a psychosis, a neurosis, or a character disorder. I believe that suicide is more accurately seen as a more-or-less transient psychological constriction, involving our emotions and intellect. "There was nothing else to do." "The only way out was death." "The only thing I could do [was to kill myself,]

and the only way to do it was to jump from something good and high." Those are examples of the constricted mind at work.

Synonyms for constriction are a tunneling or a focusing or narrowing of the range of options usually available to *that* individual's consciousness when the mind is not panicked into dichotomous (either-or) thinking. Either I achieve this specific (almost magical) happy solution *or* I cease to be. All or nothing.

The sad and dangerous fact is that in a state of constriction, the usual life-sustaining responsibilities toward loved ones are not merely disregarded; much worse, they are sometimes not even within the range of what is in the mind. A person who commits suicide turns off all ties to the past, declares a kind of mental bankruptcy, and his or her memories have no lien. Those memories can no longer save him; he is beyond their reach. Any attempt at rescue has to deal, from the first, with the suicidal person's psychological constriction. The challenge and the task are clear: Open up the possibilities; widen the perceptual blinders.

8. The common *action* in suicide is *escape* or egression. Egression is a person's intended departure from a region, often a region of distress. From the suicide notes: "So I'll get out by taking my life." "Now, at last, freedom from the mental torment." Suicide is the ultimate egression, besides which running away from home, quitting a job, deserting an army, or leaving a spouse—all egressions or escapes—pale in comparison. We speak of "unplugging" the world when we go on vacation or bury ourselves in a good book, but most of us distinguish between the wish to get away for a while and the desire to shut out life forever.

9. The common *interpersonal act* in suicide is *communication of intention*. One of the most interesting things we have found from the psychological autopsies of unequivocal

suicidal deaths done at the Los Angeles Center was that there were clues to the impending lethal event in the vast majority of cases. "I am dying," said William Styron to a perfect stranger; Castro said, "I began to say goodbye to friends." Many individuals intent on committing suicide, albeit ambivalent about it, consciously or unconsciously, emit clues of intention, signals of distress, whimpers of helplessness, or pleas for intervention. It is a sad and paradoxical thing to note that the common interpersonal act of suicide is not hostility, not rage or destruction, not even withdrawal, not depression, but communication of intention. Of course, these verbal and behavioral communications are often indirect, but audible if one has the ears and wits to hear them.

10. The common *pattern* in suicide is consistent with *lifelong styles* of coping. People who are dying of a disease (say, cancer) over weeks or months are very much themselves, even exaggerations of their normal selves. In almost every such case, we can see, if we look, certain patterns: displays of emotion and uses of defense mechanisms consistent with that person's immediate and long-range reactions to pain, threat, failure, powerlessness, and duress that match earlier negative episodes in that life. People are enormously loyal to themselves, and they show this by the consistency of their reactions to certain aspects of life throughout its span. In suicide, however, we are initially thrown off the scent because suicide is an act which, by its definition, that individual has never done before, so there is no exact precedent. Yet there are some consistencies with how that individual has coped with previous setbacks. We must look to previous episodes of disturbance, dark times in that life, to assess the individual's capacity to endure psychological pain. We need to see whether or not there is a penchant for constriction and dichotomous thinking, a tendency to throw in the towel, for earlier paradigms of escape and egression. Information

would lie in the details and nuances of *how* jobs were quit, how spouses were divorced, and how psychological pain was managed. This repetition of a tendency to capitulate, to flee, to blot it out, to escape is perhaps the most telling single clue to an ultimate suicide.

I was once asked to participate in investigating the suicide of an old man (in his eighties), in the terminal stages of cancer, who took the tubes and needles out of himself, somehow got the bedrail down, summoned the strength to lift the heavy window in his hospital room, and threw himself out the window to his death. I puzzled over him (as I do over all suicides). What was his great hurry? If he had done nothing, he would have been dead in a few days. He was a veteran of World War II and there was a full record on him. The relatively few "social" (occupational, marital, educational, military) facts were especially illuminating. This was a man married several times. sparsely educated, a rather itinerant fellow who was never fired by a boss or divorced by a spouse. Rather, it was *he* who quit the job before he was fired. His wives did not walk out on him; he left them. Before a possible court martial, he got himself transferred. His life seemed like a series of precipitous departures. Death by cancer was not going to get him; he would die in his own way, when he decided. In 20/20 retrospect, his suicide seemed totally predictable from an extrapolation of his character.

To repeat: People are very consistent with themselves. But I hasten to add that no possible future suicide is set in stone, and the capacity for change is our great hallmark as human beings. It is probably next to impossible to behave "out of character," but what is possible, and happens all the time, is for changes in character—growth and maturity—to occur, and for transiently overwhelming psychache to be resisted and survived.

Some of our most beloved novels weave suicide into their plots. I am thinking of Kate Chopin's *The Awakening*, Flaubert's *Madame Bovary*, Goethe's *The Sorrows of Young Werther*, Lagerqvist's *The Dwarf*, Tolstoy's *Anna Karenina*, to name a handful. What is interesting about them (aside from their gorgeous writing) is the consistency of the chief characters, and our acceptance of their deaths as almost-fitting endings to their lives. The suicidal outcome is not a De Maupassant-like surprise, but rather an understandable outcome within the confines of that character, a lamentable but psychological "necessity," given the unhappy circumstances and unhappy deficiencies of that person. Can anybody commit suicide? Not likely. But if you are an Anna or an Emma or an Edna, then you must be very careful how you turn life's pages and into what corners you paint yourself.

There are also certain questions we might pose to help get a person out of a constricted suicidal state: Where do you hurt? What is going on? What is it that you feel you have to solve or get out of? Do you have any formed plans to do anything harmful to yourself, and what might those plans be? What would it take to keep you alive? Have you ever before been in a situation in any way similar to this, and what did you do and how was it resolved?

You should be thinking how to help the suicidal person generate alternatives to suicide, first by rethinking (and restating) the problem, and then by looking at possible other courses of action. New conceptualizations may not totally solve the problem the way it was formulated, but they can offer a solution the person can live with. And that is the primary goal of working with a suicidal person.

8

Matching the Therapy to the Individual's Needs

Let us talk for awhile about psychotherapy.

The implications of the 10 commonalities for a suicidal patient in therapy should be fairly obvious: Reduce the pain; remove the blinders; lighten the pressure—all three, even just a little bit. To put it technically (in terms of perturbation and lethality), if you address the individual's perturbation (the sense of things being wrong), that person's lethality (the pressure to get out of it by suicide) will decrease as the perturbation is reduced. That is the goal of therapy with a suicidal person. Within reason, anything that works—including medications and the sanctuary of hospitalization—should be used, if the prescriber knows what he or she is doing.

It is important to think about and talk about alternatives to suicide, first to rethink and restate the problem and look at possible courses of action other than a suicidal solution. While these new conceptualizations will not totally solve the problem the way the suicidal person may have formulated it, they will provide options of other nonlethal ways of viewing the (redefined) problems.

Psychotherapy is a special arena, unlike any other, a place for special explorations and personal growth. All sorts of interesting and beneficial things can happen in psychotherapy. Within the one goal of saving the patient, there are two stages toward achieving that goal. The first stage is adjusting or directing the therapy to match that person's particular disposition of psychological needs. This is an achievable goal, which requires only the skill and flexibility of the therapist and the active cooperation of the patient. The second goal—the long-range, hoped-for outcome of therapy—is nothing less than re-examining and altering the life-threatening needs themselves.

If we examine any ordinary conversation between two co-equal participants, we see that a number of things are going on. There is an unspoken set of mutually agreed on rules or maneuvers that are operating during the flow of talk. For example, the two speakers seemed to have agreed to take turns or permit interruptions. In my childhood, at the animated family dinner-table, it seemed to be a rule that no one should ever get to complete a sentence; when I was at Harvard, that rule was quite different. Other unspoken rules might be: to change the subject, to enlarge on a subject, to change the mood, to digress, to ask for information, to terminate the conversation, among others.

The main content of conversations around the world is on manifest items—that is, people are talking about what they appear to be talking about: babies, food, money, political events, personalities in the news, families, automobiles, and so on and on. When a friend asks you about what gasoline mileage you get in your new car, those are the topics: cars and mileage.

On the other hand, psychotherapy is not a mere conversation. To be sure, it has its own rules, but they are different. Fundamentally, therapy differs from conversation in at least two important ways: It is hierarchical; that is, therapist and patient are not co-equal; they cannot, as in a conversation, trade information, take equal time, or exchange places. Their roles are quite different. The other difference between a conversation and psychotherapy is in the content of the talk. It is not just about cars and mileage. In therapy, there is an implicit understanding between the two parties that the patient will (at least occasionally) talk about things ordinarily not mentioned, and even about things that have never before come to mind. The paradox of psychotherapy is that the patient comes voluntarily to talk about things he or she doesn't ordinarily want to discuss, including those never even thought of before. The greater paradox is not that this is done, but that it turns out to be helpful.

In psychotherapy, there are what I call "maneuvers" that the therapist can use to move the process along. Of course, the topic of psychotherapy has its own lexicon, its own technical vocabulary of indispensable terms like transference, resistance, mechanisms of defense, and so on—hundreds of textbooks seem to be required to define these terms—but this is not the place for such a major digression. Here I have limited myself to listing some two-dozen of these maneuvers whose purpose is to craft the therapy to reflect the specific needs of a particular patient. Table 4 presents a list of these maneuvers. The aim of this approach is to tailor the pattern

Table 4 Psychotherapeutic Maneuvers

1.	ESTABLISH	13.	IDENTIFY
2.	FOCUS ON	14.	EMPHASIZE
3.	AVOID	15.	MONITOR
4.	BE ALERT FOR	16.	CONTACT
5.	ENCOURAGE	17.	EXPLORE
6.	REINFORCE	18.	INTERPRET
7.	BE AWARE OF	19.	BE WARY OF
8.	RESIST	20.	EVALUATE
9.	DISAGREE WITH	21.	ASSESS
10.	EXPLAIN	22.	OBTAIN
11.	INSTITUTE	23.	CONSULT WITH
12.	ARRANGE FOR	24.	RULE OUT

Note: These maneuvers can be tailored to each individual, and each maneuver can be related to frustrated psychological needs.

or cut the template to fit *that* individual's disposition of psychological needs, the needs causing the pain that drives the suicide.

Here is an excerpt from a sesssion with Beatrice Bessen, our bright, suicidal college student. As you read it, look for the counteractive elements in her assertions and responses.

Beatrice: I'm very interested in the things you're talking about. I have personal doubts about some of the theories. In studying psychology, I have always had my doubts about certain areas I've come across. I think most people do in studying anything. But I'm interested. And I think I can give you honest answers about what I've been through and what it feels like to be inside my head.

ES: Tell me more about your psychological pain.

BB: I think so. Yeah. All my pain has been more

mental than anything else. I've always had a a hard time crying or screaming or being emotional, running around and throwing myself about, whatever. But logically I had spent time thinking and depicting and analyzing myself to a point where I would feel insane. I can talk myself into a trap in my head. I think my doubts come from whether or not people can change. Change fundamental things, that is. I, myself, have changed after going through college, as opposed to the person I was in high school. The person I am now, those kinds of things change. But I feel there are fundamental things that I have never been able to change, but wanted to. So I have some doubts about the whole theory that you can just change these opinions that people have of the world.

ES: Can you describe one of those fundamental things which you don't think can change?

BB: Fully trusting anybody.

ES: Fully?

BB: Completely. Unconditionally. And I mean even trusting yourself completely.
[Pause.]

ES: What are you thinking about right now?

BB: I'm thinking about extremes. And how my tendency is to go for all or nothing.

ES: What? To dichotomize the world?

BB: Some things aren't as obvious though. Being abused, physically battered by somebody would be easy to see. And I think pesonally it would be easy for me to see and I would get out, call the police, whatever, take action. But I think there are complex ways that people beat each other up, that are not physical and you can't see.

ES: Absolutely. But there are also exaggerations that one makes, especially about the past.

BB: I don't feel that my past is really gone, or that

my past is away from me, or that it's a time behind
me. I feel like it's here all the time, it's in the now,
that it's just as present. I mean I recognize that it
was past, but it doesn't feel that way.

ES: Is it posssible for you to see the past in a slightly
different way? That your view of it wasn't the only
possible view of it? That it may not have been as
dire as you thought it was?

BB: Sure. I think it is, logically. But I've logically
talked myself out of any kind of destruction, but it
doesn't stay. Because when the trauma happened,
when I was eight years old or whatever, at the time
it felt like life or death. And even though now, as an
educated adult in my twenties, I can look back and
say, well, logically, that wasn't a life-or-death situation, but at the time I didn't know that. As an adult
you do, but as an eight year old, you don't. So, as an
adult you recognize where this fear comes from, you
have analyzed your past and put your past behind
you, so to speak, and logically understand your life
is not threatened, and you try to take control of the
situation as an adult. You know how to take precau-
tions because the little eight year old might pop up.
I do this all the time, to protect myself, but the controls that I use, the ways I set up the situation so
that I can handle it in case the little child in me pops
up and thinks it's a life-or-death thing, these controls
that I'm using are also life threatening. I just can't
live like that every day. I just can't live in such extreme fear, this am I going to die or am I going to
live state of mind. It's too hard. So I use controls.
But unfortunately, and I don't think by accident, I
have picked controls that are, eventually, deadly.

ES: Can you say what they are?

BB: For me, currently, it's dieting. But it's been other
things. I think it's addictions. I've used drugs.

I've fantasized about suicide obsessively, all the time. And I wasn't going to die from thinking, but I think there was an eventual destruction because the goal was to fulfill those fantasies.

ES: And how was that?

BB: Various ways. It was over a period of three or four years where I was fantasizing every single day, so that each night before I went to bed I thought of different ways. One example was to bleed to death. I had it stuck in my mind, probably a lot of adolescents do, that bleeding was poetic and tragic. So I would imagine bleeding to death, slowly. That was one of the ways. It was somehow romantic and related to love. There were songs and books connected with it. I was very immersed in it, in songs and poems I was writing myself. The songs that I was composing and everything in my life were part of this gothic theme. It was a control thing, because I was using all that mind energy, that obsessing, to avoid what was really going on. It was an addiction. I think that ends up being destructive in and of itself, like adopting the tranquilizers every time you get nervous and every time you feel scared. To be dependent on them, and on people.

ES: And why is that so bad?

BB: I agree with you that people need to be dependent, and that pop psychology has taken co-dependency too far, but I'm talking about something severe. I would use another person the way I use dieting now, as a way to keep that fear at bay. I would use them to a point where you wouldn't be able to call it humanly, nicely dependent. To the point where the other person is telling me to back off. I couldn't see the line between him and me, where we were different people. I don't think it was healthy at all. Using controls like that are problems in themselves. I'm talking about not letting those things go. Ever. Excessively. Being afraid of not using the tranquilizers. Being afraid of not letting go of the other person's hand. . . .

Let us now look to how this approach of using the 24 psychological maneuvers might be applied more generally, specifically to our three suicidal people, Ariel, Beatrice, and Castro. (Only one of them, Castro, had actually been my patient.) While writing this book, I sought out consultation on these cases, as I might have done if I were actually treating them as patients. Fortunately, there was an ideal consultant just down the hall from me in the UCLA Neuropsychiatric Institute (my academic home since 1970). In a series of consultations, Dr. Robert O. Pasnau, Professor of Psychiatry at UCLA and former President of the American Psychiatric Association, studied the cases of Ariel, Beatrice, and Castro and reviewed with me how one might have used the list of verbs to organize the (imaginary) therapeutic dialogues. The intention was to tailor these maneuvers for each of these three people. My sessions with Dr. Pasnau were, so to speak, a series of postmortem psychotherapeutic consultations for the purpose of my understanding better how the theory might have fitted the practice—if the opportunties had been present for therapeutic sessions with Ariel and Beatrice.

I present six (of the 24) psychotherapeutic maneuvers here to give an idea of how all this works. Notice how the details of the therapy flow from (and are consistent with) the patient's primary frustrated psychological needs—how they are tailor-made for Ariel's need to be loved, Beatrice's need for counteraction, and Castro's need for affiliation. These six illustrative maneuevers have been picked almost at random.

ESTABLISH.   Let us begin with the first maneuver, *es-*

tablish, as good a place as any to start. It is obvious that the therapist would, of course, wish to establish a good working relationship with each patient, to establish rapport. But establishing rapport is not a perfunctory thing. From the patient's point of view, it is enormously important. At rock bottom, rapport (with a frightened, isolated suicidal person) may mean that he or she is not alone in the world, and not totally abandoned.

In psychotherapy, there is a relationship that is more intense and more powerful than rapport. It is called transference, specifically positive transference, by which is meant the shift or flow of feelings of trust and warmth and benign expectation with regard to another person. This other individual is often a person in authority like a doctor or a teacher (or even a cult leader). "Here," you say to the benign-looking, competent-acting doctor in the emergency room, "Take care of me," or to the inspiring teacher, "Teach me. Tell me what to do." To the therapist, "Help me to become less unhappy. Take care of me."

Ariel's almost immediate positive transference to me—her need to come up to me after a lecture and her eagerness to make some special, intimate tapes especially for me—all this is important to note. It might certainly have been used to her advantage if there had been an opportunity for psychotherapy with her. In that setting, she might have worked on (and improved) some of her tangled and worrisome relationships with her real, dead father, by examining the nuances of her present reactions to the therapist. This process might have been applied not only to the things she said in therapy but also to the things she realistically and unrealistically projected and fantasized in the "real" world. And then there would have been an opportunity for her to test these ideas both in the special reality of the therapy consultation room and the relationships in her real life.

With Beatrice, the problem *is* the transference—namely, her lifelong inability really to trust any adult figure. If there were ever therapy with her, the therapist would have to expect only tepidness on the positive side, and emphasis on the negative transference manifesting itself in mistrust and subtle criticism. Here is an excerpt from an interview with her:

Beatrice: I have definitely slowed down my pace from adolescence, without a doubt. My life is boring in comparison. But I find that it isn't safe. It's like I'm in surgery without tranquilizers or without someone's hand to hold. I'm only comfortable living in the extremes.

ES: Do you aspire to change that?

BB: Yes, of course. Because I've discovered that living in the extremes is dangerous.

ES: You seem to have this fascinating need for excitement, for drama, for its own sake. For you to do otherwise seems so dull to you. Having felt abandoned, you've turned to extremes to entertain yourself, to feel some kind of life in yourself. It's too interesting for you to throw away.

BB: Well, that depends. I don't believe that when you die you become null, nonexistent. I believe that energy changes form, but doesn't die. That's a whole other big issue. It's interesting to consider what people who try to commit suicide think about death.

ES: Isn't suicide a way of throwing your life away? Of denying the integrity that you have had as a person?

BB: So?

ES: What do you mean, "so"?

BB: Well, if you really wanted to commit suicide, I don't think it would matter, your whole life's work. If you are saying that you, personally, can't do it in order to keep your status with everybody around, I think if you were in the position to really kill yourself you wouldn't care. Actually, people might take you more seriously, that you really knew something about suicidality; that you had an insight.

ES: Do you think you will still believe this when you are 40?

BB: I don't think I'll make it to 40 if I'm still thinking this way. I don't think I'd bother. . . .

You can see that doing therapy with Beatrice would be an against-her-grain struggle from the start.

Turning to our third person: Castro's lifelong search for his missing father is poignantly reflected in his ambivalent, mostly positive transference to me. His most honorific word for me is "friend." A trustworthy elder sibling figure, a mentor, was the most that he could aspire to find. Was there anyone in his life he ever called "Father"?

From the therapist's view, the wonderful thing about positive transference is that the therapist doesn't have to earn it; it is projected by the patient. All the therapist needs to do is to act so that he or she continues to deserve it.

AVOID.   The third maneuver, *Avoid*, is an important consideration in many cases. In separate sessions with me, Dr. Pasnau was clear about the different things that should be avoided in therapy with the three people we have looked at. For Ariel, he suggested that in approaching her one should avoid criticizing her family or getting into any kind of conflict with her mother. Independence (from her family) was not the main goal for Ariel, certainly not at the beginning of therapy. Her need to be loved as part of the family was much more important. Amicability and affection were the proper prescriptions.

For Beatrice, becoming her administrator (in case of the advisability of hospitalization) or becoming the chief limit-

setter in her life was to be avoided. She brings enough counteraction into the therapy without its being exacerbated by
the therapist.

As for Castro, the topic of his homosexuality should be
avoided until (and unless) he initiates an overt discussion of
it. The exact sexual nature of his relationships with the people he mentions should not be queried. In what he talks (or
writes) about, he is the boss and sets the agenda. He is eager
to communicate, and he will come to every topic by-and-by.
The therapist should avoid the appearance of pushing him.
The therapist's task is to *affiliate* with Castro; be on the same
side; not threaten him or feed him any ideas before he is
ready to digest them. In general, it is best to let the patient
set the pace, especially around taboo topics.

TO BE AWARE OF.   What does it mean to *Be aware
of*? In my view, the therapist should be aware of Ariel's need
for affection and approval. Not phony approbation, but genuine acceptance. The therapist should have a good modicum
of positive countertransference toward Ariel; should like her
and genuinely want to help her, keeping her psychological
needs in mind.

Of course, Ariel's problems can be conceptualized in different ways. If she had visited the average psychiatric facility
as a patient (before her immolation), she would have been
diagnosed in terms of the American Psychiatric Association's
Diagnostic and Statistical Manual for Mental Disorders, in
part, so that she might be eligible for third-party payments.
In those settings, it is likely that she would have been given
diagnostic labels such as endogenous depression, borderline
patient (with unrealistic and inexhaustible demands for attention and love), immaturity reaction, and narcissistic disorder. Medications for these diagnoses would have been
given to her. (And they might have helped.) That is what is
ordinarily done.

But the therapist would still have other issues to deal with; not only the underlying psychological pain, but the needs that would have remained even after taking Prozac or any other drug. Once a person is out of the woods, so to speak, no longer in danger of hurting the self or others, the therapist ought to initiate and develop a dialogue with the person so that both of them can learn, in admittedly different ways, the mental landscape of the beleaguered person. I have been convinced that psychological needs are foremost in understanding suicidal people. Thus, my job is to establish a relationship to find out how these needs can shape Ariel's, or anyone else's, personality. Drug treatment and psychotherapy can work hand in hand. Ideally, the psychiatric facility or ward or consultation office should be a place where suicidal individuals can come and be assessed and treated and, simultaneously, comforted for their psychological pain and anguish.

I deeply believe that the principal function of a mental health facility (and the staff members within it) and of psychotherapists generally—after the obvious need to protect people from their own self-destructive impulses is assured—is to assess and evaluate psychological pain as it relates to frustrated psychological needs, and then to act as *anodynes*. An anodyne is a substance that, or a person who, relieves *pain*. The psychotherapist's main function is to be anodynic; to lessen pain—for Ariel or for anyone. And we would try to be aware of (and use) anything that would help serve this function.

Our view of Beatrice is, understandably, somewhat different. With her, we would be aware of the role that her family continues to play in her life. It must have taken a highly focused determination when Beatrice was a youngster for her to feel so fiercely embattled against her parents. Or maybe she modeled herself after their combativeness. But, in any event, she must have believed herself mighty important to set up a kingdom of her own—even if the banner of that kingdom sometimes flew upside down in defeat. In an adolescent hospitalization (following her first suicide attempt), she was diagnosed (in that hospital) as having a borderline personality, an eating disorder, and an obsessive personality. No doubt accurate enough, but not reflecting her frustrated psychological needs that had been aroused and exacerbated by her parent's divorce.

There are other technical labels for Beatrice's condition, like anaclitic depression. Anaclitic means to lean on. Such dependent children and adolescents who have been abandoned are in trouble when the people they have depended on step away, and they "fall" into a depression. This seems to have happened to Beatrice, but what has also happened is that she fought back, in a battle contained mostly within her own mind and her own body.

Beatrice's frustrated need for counteraction—her need to leave before the other person possibly abandons her—gave her enormous pain that she tried to treat with occasional assaults on her own body—her anorexia and suicide attempts. This is an instance where the problem is her own difficulty with basic trust. Establishing a working relationship with her (to do the psychological tests and so on) was, in fact, easy and pleasant for me, but creating a lasting positive transference might be an uphill climb against her deeply ingrained inclinations.

We can see that Beatrice is civilized, well-mannered, able to get along. But—and this is the nub of the problem—she has trained herself to be unable to trust and love. Can she live with a lover after *he* declares his love and wants a commitment? Her world is filled with people who aren't there for her—the psychological absence of key personnel. If you shut out everybody who tries, you may end up talking to yourself and feeling like an orphan.

As for Castro, the friend or therapist would need to be aware of his state of physical health, in light of the fact that he had not taken any solid food since the shooting and continued to lose weight and physical mass. In the last few years, he gave the impression of utter fatigue and a growing sense of weakness that was not at all present in the few years following the shooting. Something more to be aware of and to be concerned about, and to monitor.

DISAGREE WITH.   Should we *disagree with* the suicidal person? Disagreeing with a patient is a dicey and worrisome thing, but the fact is that some basic disagreements with the patient are fundamental to psychotherapy. (Disagreeing does not mean argument or disputation.) One always fundamentally disagrees with a suicidal person; you don't say, "Why, yes, I agree that you ought to kill yourself." On the contrary, you recognize that the person is there because he or she is sufficiently ambivalent and some important part wants to find a way to live. So that disagreement, as a maneuver, has a fundamental place in therapy.

Here are some of Dr. Pasnau's suggestions on this topic. He would disagree with Ariel's account of her fantasizing her father was dead before she found him. What she reports (about knowing he was dead before she saw him dead) is probably a retrospectively altered false memory, reflecting her anxiety, contrition, and guilt over his suicide. As a parallel goal, the therapy should aim to mollify her guilt over his suicide, which was probably motivated by his own private frustrations and pains.

With Beatrice, one would disagree with her argument for making a worst-case scenario of her relationships and then making that worst-case pattern come true. If she were in therapy, one would look carefully, detail by detail, at how she formed a relationship and how she subtly guided its course so that its outcome would be negative and her suspicions confirmed. Perhaps there is room for some fine tuning of how she lives out this pattern.

With Castro, of course, I actually had the opportunity to interact, and, on occasion, disagree. This took the form of a kind of intellectual discussion. One item was my pointing out to him how he cast his relationships, especially his love relationships, in terms of war. He was a general, and it was a battle. His imagery was martial. (That is what attracted him to the Caesars.) What came to my mind was De Rougemont's stimulating but not always dependable book *Love in the Western World*, especially the chapter on love and war. I actually obtained a copy from the university library and meant to discuss it with Castro, but other more important things were then happening with him and there was never an appropriate moment for it. He had to come from hundreds of miles away to the university hospital for relatively brief intervals for his reparative surgeries (when I could see him). The remainder of our interactions was by mail and, considering his speech handicap, by very occasional telephone calls.

ARRANGE FOR.   Is there anything we can *arrange for* these persons? With suicidal patients especially, I believe that an important part of the therapist's task (or the task of any friend) is to act as an ombudsman—a person who does practical things for the patient, who runs interference as it were, and helps with some of the onerous details of life. This is nothing new. The only special feature I am adding here, consistent with my overall beliefs, is that these practical extensions of the therapy should be consistent with the patient's needs. Dr. Pasnau's comments fitted in perfectly with this approach. For Ariel, one night arrange to talk to her mother and possibly set up a joint meeting with Ariel and her mother. For Beatrice, make sure that there is especially good coverage if there were ever an occasion when the therapist needed to skip some sessions (or during vacation) and supply her with the therapist's itinerary and telephone paging numbers. Treat an absence seriously. In relation to Castro, one should arrange for social service follow-up, and make contacts with the Braille Institute for books on tape, and with his local community college, among others.

TO BE WARY OF. What should we *be wary of*? In therapy, vigilance is the name of the game. One should always be wary of increases in the person's lethality, in cryptic remarks that might imply suicide ("I can't live like this"), and not hesitate to ask directly about them. Within the flow of therapy, we might be wary of giving Ariel the impression of feeling sorry for her, avoiding anything that might rob her of her dignity. In this same vein, we should be wary of Beatrice's believing the current popular explanations of anorexia, such as recently recovered "memories" of earlier sexual exploitation by an adult. And with Castro, we would need to be aware (and try constantly to share this awareness with him) of his tendency to recreate a no-win relationship with yet another sexual partner.

The act of reading itself can be a special experience and a mental and even spiritual experience. As you read along and think about people mentioned in these pages, you can simultaneously think of yourself and others you care about. In thinking about Ariel, Beatrice, and Castro, I hope you have put yourself (or a relative or friend or acquaintance) momentarily in their shoes. Or, if you have ever known someone who has contemplated suicide, you might think now about what were his or her pressing psychological needs? How would you fill in the Need Form? (What weightings would you give yourself?) How would you fill in the content for each of these 24 maneuvers for that person you are worried about? Or for yourself? And, if there are any conditions under which you yourself think of suicide, how might you approach a friend or therapist for help?

The purpose of this book is to stimulate you to think about these matters. I invite readers to examine these maneuvers—and the needs and the commonalities—and see what might flow from such an introspective adventure. Since each of us is unique, we must come to terms with our own demons, our own fears, and the terms under which we can live out our days. It is always advantageous to be armed with as much information about ourselves as it is reasonably possible to acquire. On the topic of suicide, knowledge is powerfully preventive.

9

Final Thoughts and Reflections

The suicidal act is both a moving away and a moving toward. Psychache, psychological pain, is what the individual wishes to escape; peace is what the person seeks and moves toward. In suicide, the two goals are merged as one: Escape from pain *is* relief—that is how peace is defined. The unbearable pain is transformed into peace; the suffering is taken away. At least, that is what the suicidal person thinks and hopes.

To a suicidal individual, to be unconscious means to be in a state of tranquil quiet, a nothingness and oblivion that is total and complete. Problems are not merely taken care of; there are no problems, and, even better, there is no consciousness of the possibility of problems—or of anything else.

Suicide is an effort to "get away from it all." It is the ultimate escape. Jean Baechler, a contemporary French social scientist, in his book *Suicides* discusses "escapist suicides" as the centerpiece of his presentation. "To commit a suicide of flight is to escape by taking one's own life from a situation sensed by the subject to be intolerable."[1] The action of suicide is an exiting, a departure from a painful life. The act of suicide says: In case of fire (of unbearable negative emotions) use this Exit.

Even in Hell this is so. A concentration-camp prisoner wrote about his thoughts while in the camp: "I look at those hanging and am jealous of the peace that they know." Speaking of Hell, by and large the idea of Hell does not ordinarily enter into suicide. On the contrary, there are some few suicides—committed out of the pain of grief—in which the idea of reunion with departed loved ones, in heaven or some other peaceful haven, is in the mind of the suicidal person. But most suicides—as is clear from reading a large number of suicide notes—are disappointingly secular. The destination (or concern) is not to *go* anywhere, except *away*. The goal is to stop the flow of intolerable consciousness; not to continue in an afterlife or an eternity. "Escape" does not mean to escape from one torture chamber to enter another. In suicide the goal is to achieve a peace of mindlessness.

The clinical problem with suicide—the challenge for the potential rescuer—is to wrestle with the fact that the goals of escape and peace *are* beguiling to the suicidal person. If they were not, the person would not be suicidal. One must recognize and deal with the fact that continuance in life is automatically burdened with returns to duty and pain.

Ever since I first read this passage as a young man, I have always admired Thomas Mann's genius for catching this life-

and-death counterpoise. The key passage is from his first novel, *Buddenbrooks*, written when he was all of 25.

> Cases of typhoid take the following course.
>
> When the fever is at its height, life calls to the patient: calls out to him as he wanders in his distant dream, and summons him in no uncertain voice. The harsh, imperious call reaches the spirit on that remote path that leads into the shadows, the coolness and peace. He hears the call of life, the clear, fresh, mocking summons to return to the distant scene which he has already left so far behind him, and already forgotten. And there may well up in him something like a feeling of shame for a neglected duty; a sense of renewed energy, courage and hope: he may recognize a bond existing still between him and that stirring, colorful, callous existence which he had thought he had left so far behind him. Then, however far he may have wandered on his distant path, he will turn back—and live. But if he shudders when he hears life's voice, if the memory of that vanished scene and the sound of that lusty summons make him shake his head, and make him put out his hand to ward off as he flies forward in the way of escape that is opened to him—then it is clear that the patient will die.[2]

That is a perfect description of the inner workings of the suicidal debate, how the awful work is actually done.

What is warded off is psychological pain. But what is critical is the individual's unwillingness to endure pain, the larger characteristics that make a person the person he or she is, the sense of identity, and especially that person's ideal self and ideal identity. In other words, how the person privately and secretly really views himself or herself. I quote here from my colleague, Robert Litman: "People commit suicide because they cannot accept their pain, because the pain does not fit in with their concept of themselves, with their personal ideal. So for me, the long-range treatment of chronically suicidal people includes helping them change their self concept so that they can learn to acknowledge that their pain, while unique to them, is not radically different from everyone else's pain, and their personhood is basically pretty much the same as everybody else's personhood."[3]

Some nonsuicidal people believe that they are pretty much the same as everybody else. But in suicide, there is often the feeling that one's pain is somehow special and greater than the pain and suffering of others, making it unendurable in a special way—bordering on a feeling of grandiosity. This is so because suicidal people tend to cut themselves off from human contact and are talking only to themselves. They think that their suffering and their dying are unique. They imagine their funeral and their mourners—in effect, an existence in this world, at least for a while, after their own death; that they will be remembered, not forgotten; that they stay alive in the minds of others.

Dying is the one thing—perhaps the only thing—in life that you don't have to do. Stick around long enough and it will be done for you. And dying is also the only thing you have to do. There is no If to death. The only questions in dying are when and where and how. Suicide names the time, the place, and the method. Suicide is the only kind of death in which the individual supplies most of the details for the death certificate. Suicide—for all the noble-born literary heroes and all the Thomas Chattertons and all the Archduke Rudolfs and all the Sylvia Plaths who have committed it—is a lonely act, a desperate and, almost always, unnecessary one. Most of us have thought about it. It touches all the social strata, the highest and the lowest, all races, both sexes, all age groups, each with its own special obligations.

Almost every one of us has serious obligations in life, but there is only one *obligatory* from which there is *no* escape— to die. Admittedly, to die well is a most difficult thing to do.

To die by suicide is to die before one's time; it almost never gets applause—except, perhaps, in grand opera. There is no "courtly suicide," with the possible exception of doing so at the request of one's liege or lord, but suicide on command is hardly the type of suicide that happens nowadays. In World War II, Field Marshall Erwin Rommel was ordered by Hitler to commit suicide, but the onus here is on the demented Hitler.

By curious contrast, the other leader of our then wartime enemy made what is perhaps the most impactful suicide *prevention* statement of this century, perhaps of recorded history. In the rescript of capitulation on August 14, 1945, in which Emperor Hirohito, by unprecedented radio broadcast—almost none of his subjects had ever heard his voice before—ordered his loyal subjects to surrender, he touched on the two main antidotes to suicide: the sense of futurity; and the redefining of the key term, variously defined by the person as unbearable, unacceptable, intolerable, unendurable. With great prescience, the Emperor commanded all members of his nation-family:

> It is according to the dictates of time and fate that we have resolved to pave the way for a grand peace for all the generations to come by enduring the unendurable and suffering what is unsufferable.[4]

He ordered his people to live.

Sometimes the most difficult thing in the world is to choose to endure life. But even when there is no choice, as in a natural death in old age, dying *well* is among the most challenging feats of life: To die with some sense of grace, panache, good manners, or thanatological breeding—especially when one is frightened and in pain—can be the crown of one's life. Of course, the physical pain can and should be treated, but there is no handy morphine drip for psychological pain that, to be effective, does not, at the same time, alter who we are. To die naturally will, in the course of time, occur to most of us, but to die "well," to accept one's mortality and not hasten one's death may be the most difficult act in a life.

To "will the obligatory"—a phrase from Otto Rank[5]—is to accept the immutable cycles of Nature, especially human nature, and to understand that (whether or not you believe that there is any existential purpose or meaning to life, or a spiritual extension beyond it) no one, absolutely no one, escapes being finite and mortal. And knowing this brute fact, then to accept it, to *will* it, and not be in an unnecessary state of angst or terror or rebellion over it can be a remarkable and in many ways a truly human feat of courage and grace.

This book propounds the view that suicide stems from psychological pain, and that that pain comes from frustrated psychological needs peculiar to each person. But the suicidal person must also have the desire or drive to escape the unbearable pain of these frustrated needs. What then is the "psychological soil" in which the suicidal mind malignantly flourishes? While we can agree on the central role of psychache, we must still speculate on the causes of the reactions of the suicidal mind. Are these predilections fostered in early childhood, or can they arise for the first time during adulthood? We know a great deal about the more or less immediate psychological circumstances that surround suicide, but there is no easy answer to the enigma of the "root causes" of a lower threshold for withstanding the psychological pains associated with suicide.

I am totally willing to believe that suicide can occur in adults who could not stand the immediate pain of grief or loss that faced them, independent of a good or bad childhood or good or bad parental care and love. But I am somewhat more inclined to hold to the view that the subsoil, the root causes of being unable to withstand those adult assaults lie in the deepest recesses of personality that are laid down in rather early childhood. In my view, these speculations are illustrated by the three clinical cases in this book.

Each of our three acquaintances—Ariel, Beatrice, and Castro—reports that they were unhappy in childhood. Those are two key words in any life: unhappy and childhood. Suicide never stems from happiness—it happens because of the stark absence of it. In this century, especially in the latter half, we tend to identify happiness with the mere absence of pain and the presence of creature comforts—good food, fine wine, expensive clothes. But in relation to *suicide*, genuine happiness has an almost magical aura to it. Or, to put it another way, unhappiness reflects the lost joys of an unrealized childhood. Early childhood especially is the time when we can—unrestrained by realistic and adult rules and actualities—fantasize about what we would optimally like to have happen within ourselves and between ourselves and our parents. Secret inner pacts can be made and savored. These fantasies give a magical quality, a special happiness, an ecstasy and consuming exuberance that one can experience only in a childhood that is essentially benign.

Those are the benchmarks; anything less than that is pain. And, once lost, or once glimpsed but never experienced, they strike in too deep, and leave such a scar that nothing can ever make them right. One feels old and burdened long before any wrinkles appear; and, as Melville said, the airs of paradise cannot erase them.[6] It is not possible to be robbed totally of one's childhood, but what does happen can seem to be just as bad. One can have one's childhood vandalized. Perhaps—I do not know—every person who commits suicide, at *any* age, has been a victim of a vandalized childhood, in which that preadolescent child has been psychologically mugged or sacked, and has had psychological needs, important to *that* child, trampled on and frustrated by malicious, preoccupied, or obtuse adults. I tend to believe that, at rock-bottom, the pains that drive suicide relate primarily not to the precipitous absence of equanimity or happiness in adulthood, but to the haunting losses of childhood's special joys.

The role of parents, relatives, friends, physicians, therapists, artisans, helpers, and good samaritans—and even books—in life is clear to everyone. We could not get through life without the help of others. But after infancy, a vast part of life is a do-it-yourself proposition. It is not inaccurate to assert that even in the best of therapies, the patient's role—the don't-do-it-yourself part of it—is vital to the success of the whole process. In this spirit I invite the reader (as has been implicit throughout this book) to reflect, to examine your own needs, how your mind is in dialogue with those ongoing needs, and to generate the self-help that might flow from such introspective insight, aided by the conceptual tools provided in these pages.

Having just asserted that each of us has to play a vital role in keeping ourselves alive, it is not, in my view, a contradiction now to say that there are times in life when we cannot do some vital things for ourselves and it is prudent on those occasions to seek the help of others. One of the themes of this book is that there is much we can do to understand our own tendencies, thoughts, and impulses toward suicide in an effort to turn those self-destructive impulses into lifesaving self-knowledge. A big part of what we can do for ourselves is to get appropriate professional help when we need it—to recognize that certain crises we cannot effectively handle alone.

The happy fact is that there are thousands of people who have been helped, their lives saved, by the intervention of therapy by psychologists, psychiatrists, physicians, suicide prevention workers, and others. It would be a sad misreading of this book to believe that—in relation to suicide and its admittedly dire consequences—there is not a large place for realistic hope of a life-prolonging outcome.

In this book, I have proposed the view that suicide is prevented by changing our perception of the situation, and by redefining what is unbearable. Perceiving that there are other possible ways of seeing things, redefining the impossible, bearing the unbearable, swallowing the undigestible bolus of shame or guilt. What has saved Beatrice Bessen is her willingness, albeit reluctant, to consider the possibility of renegotiating her perception of her parents and rethinking their role in her life.

Here, in the United States, we have never had a Sun-God Emperor or a tyrannical dictator to whom we have been taught total obedience from childhood, and whose every order we must unhesitatingly obey. Each of us is our own monarch. As long as we are alive, we democrats can say, as Melville did, "The queenly personality lives in me, and feels her royal rights." What we are talking about here is our conscience, our selves, our view of what amount of psychological pain we will put up with. It is our independent personhood, whose voice we follow, and if, in the flux of things, she orders us to die, we are doomed—unless an autonomous part of us can summon the will and the energy to answer, "I don't have to do it," or someone else, a friend or acquaintance, restrains our hand and guides us to help.

Every single instance of suicide is an action by the dictator or emperor of your mind. But in every case of suicide, the person is getting bad advice from a part of that mind, the inner chamber of councilors, who are temporarily in a panicked state and in no position to serve the person's best long-range interests. Then it is time to reach outside your own imperial head and seek more qualified and measured advice from other voices who, out of their loyalty to your larger social self, will throw in on the side of life, and—to use a Japanese image—will urge the chrysanthemum, not the sword.

All this is consistent with deep beliefs I have held for years. Suicide involves both inner disturbance and the idea of death as escape. But it is simply good sense not to commit an irrevocable suicide during a transient perturbation in the mind. Suicide is not the thing to do when you are disturbed and your thinking is constricted. There is a short aphorism or maxim that captures this lifesaving truth: Never kill yourself while you are suicidal. You can, if you must, think about suicide as much as your mind wishes and let the thought of suicide—the possibility that you could do it—carry you through the dark night. Night after night. Day after day, until the thought of self-destruction runs its course, and a fresh view of your own frustrated needs comes into clearer focus in your mind and you can, at last, pursue the realistic aspects, however dire, of your natural life.

NOTES

Chapter 1

1. Ronald Melzack and Joel Katz, The McGill Pain Questionnaire: Appraisal and Current Status. In D. C. Turk and R. Melzack (Eds.), *Handbook of Pain Assessment*. New York: Guilford Press, 1992, p. 156.

2. Eric Cassell. *The Nature of Suffering and the Goals of Medicine*. New York: Oxford University Press, 1991.

3. David B. Morris. *The Culture of Pain* Berkeley and Los Angeles: University of California Press, 1991.

4. William James. *The Varieties of Religious Experience*. New York: Longmans, Green & Co., 1902, p. 501.

5. William James. *Principles of Psychology*. New York: Henry Holt & Co., 1890.

6. Aldous Huxley. *Eyeless in Gaza*. New York: Harper & Bros., 1936. p. 365.

7. Donald O. Hebb. *The Organization of Behavior*. New York: John Wiley & Sons, 1949.

8. Henry A. Murray. *Explorations in Personality*. New York: Oxford University Press, 1938.

Chapter 2

1. Henry A. Murray. *Explorations in Personality*. New York: Oxford University Press, p. 181.
2. Forrest Robinson. *Love's Story Told: A Life of Henry A. Murray*. Cambridge, MA: Harvard University Press, 1992.

Chapter 3

1. William Styron. An Interior Pain That Is All but Indescribable, *Newsweek*, April 18, 1994, p. 52.
2. A. Alvarez. *The Savage God: A Study of Suicide*. New York: Random House, 1972.
3. Boris Pasternak. *I Remember: Sketch for an Autobiography*. New York: Pantheon, 1959.
4. Karl A. Menninger. *Man against Himself*. New York: Harcourt, Brace & Co., 1938.
5. Henry A. Murray. Dead to the World: The Passions of Herman Melville. In E. Shneidman (Ed.), *Endeavors in Psychology: Selections from the Personology of Henry A. Murray*. New York: Harper & Row, 1981.

Chapter 4

1. Henry A. Murray. *Explorations in Personality*. New York: Oxford University Press, 1938, pp. 195–197.
2. Henry A. Murray. *Thematic Apperception Test—Manual*. Cambridge, MA: President and Fellows of Harvard College, 1943.
3. Elder Olson, "Directions to the Armorer." *New Yorker*, November 14, 1959.

Chapter 5

1. Lewis M. Terman. *Genetic Studies of Genius*. Vol. I. Stanford: Stanford University Press, 1925. There have been several subsequent studies of the Terman Study of Gifted Children by Terman, Oden, Sears, Hastorf, and others.
2. Edwin Shneidman. Perturbation and Lethality as Precursors

of Suicide in a Gifted Group. *Life-Threatening Behavior*, Vol. 1, 1971, 23–45.

Chapter 6

1. Herman Melville. *Moby-Dick*. New York: Harper & Bros., 1891. Chapter 27: ". . . each *Isolato* living on a separate continent by himself."

2. Henry A. Murray. *Explorations in Personality*. New York: Oxford University Press, 1938, pp. 173–177.

3. Denis De Rougemont. *Love in the Western World*. New York: Harcourt, Brace & Co., 1940.

Chapter 7

1. Edwin Shneidman. *Definition of Suicide*. New York: John Wiley & Sons, 1985.

Chapter 9

1. Jean Baechler. *Suicides*. New York: Basic Books, 1979, p. 66.

2. Thomas Mann. *Buddenbrooks*. New York: Alfred A. Knopf, 1952. (Originally published in 1901.) Part XI, Ch. 3.

3. Robert E. Litman. Personal communication. May 13, 1995.

4. Harold A. Hanson, John G. Herndon, and William G. Langsdorf (Eds.), *Fighting for Freedom: Historic Documents*. Philadelphia: John C. Winston Co., 1947, p. 358.

5. Otto Rank. *Art and the Artist*. New York: Alfred A. Knopf, 1932.

6. Herman Melville. *Redburn*. New York: Harper & Bros., 1849, Ch. II. Moody, stricken Melville expressed his lament and his psychological insights, at age 29:

> Cold, bitter cold as December and bleak as its blasts, seemed the world then to me; there is no misanthrope like a boy disappointed; and such was I with the warm soul of me flogged out by adversity. . . . Talk not of the bitterness of

middle-age and after life; a boy can feel all that, and much more, when upon his young soul the mildew has fallen; and the fruit, which with others is only blasted after ripeness, with him is nipped in the first blossom and bud. And never again can such blights be made good; they strike in too deep, and leave such a scar that the air of Paradise might not erase it.

RECOMMENDED READINGS

The shorter the list, the more the impact. Given that there are hundreds of books on suicide, after searching my mind, and examining this and that volume in my hands, I have chosen two very special books.

1. George Howe Colt. *The Enigma of Suicide*. New York: Summit Books, 1991.

This is a recent, hefty book by a Harvard-trained journalist who interviewed several hundred suicidal people, survivors, and therapists over a 10-year period and wrote a fascinating history and account of what suicide is and how suicide prevention is actually practiced. It is the best, easy-to-read, comprehensive book written by a lay person for the lay reader with which to enter the world of "suicidology."

2. John T. Maltsberger and Mark J. Goldblatt (Eds.). *Essential Papers on Suicide*. New York: New York University Press, 1996.

This marvelous volume is both the most recent and by far the most comprehensive "reader" on suicide, especially its psychological aspects. There are 40 selections, technical articles from the psychological and psychiatric literature, from the early twentieth century to the most current journals. All the "classical" papers are here. A *must* reference book for the serious student who wishes to review the technical literature.

Plus—four easily available, superbly written suicide case histories:

1. American: Kate Chopin's *The Awakening* (1899). Suicide by walking into the ocean.
2. French: Flaubert's *Madame Bovary* (1856). Suicide by ingesting arsenic poison.
3. German: Goethe's *The Sorrows of Young Werther* (1774). Suicide by pistol bullet.
4. Russian: Tolstoy's *Anna Karenina* (1878). Suicide by throwing herself under the wheels of a train.

Anyone who reads these books will know a great deal about suicide.

APPENDIX A

*Psychological Pain Survey**

Name **Beatrice**

Sex **F** Age **20** Date _____

Definition of Psychological Pain. Psychological pain is *not* the same as bodily or physical pain. It is how you feel as a person; how you feel in your mind. It refers to how much you hurt as a human being. It is mental suffering; mental torment. It is called *psychache* (sĭk-āk). Psychache refers to hurt, anguish, soreness, aching, misery—in the mind. It is the pain of excessively felt shame, or guilt, or humiliation, or loneliness, or loss, or sadness, or dread of growing old or of dying badly, or the like. When it is felt, its introspective reality is undeniable.

The purpose of this survey is—with your help—to develop new insights into the nature of psychological pain and to try to measure it.

First of all, please rate your psychache as of *now*—how you are feeling this week—from 1 (least psychological pain) to 9 (the highest psychological pain imaginable). Circle one number:

| 1 | 2 | ③ | 4 | 5 | 6 | 7 | 8 | 9 |

*Copyright © 1993 by Edwin S. Shneidman.
Note to the reader: You may obtain permission to use this form with patients or clients by writing to Oxford University Press. Permission to reprint a few copies for self-use or use with family or friends is given herewith.

An Example of Psychache.   Instances of psychache occur every minute of every day, all over the world. Please read this vignette. The place: A Nazi concentration camp; the time: 1940.

She and her two young sons had somehow managed to survive up to that point.

One day, outside the barracks, a particularly fiendish SS officer, with a silver death's-head insignia on his military cap, suddenly grabbed her and brutally pushed her to the ground. He then quickly held up in the air her two sons, aged four and six, one in each of his massive hands. They were crying and yelling, their eyes wide with wild fear: "Momma! Momma!"

Choose, bitch," he said, "which one shall I kill?"

"What do you ask?" she screamed. "They are my children, my life! I cannot choose between them!"

"You must choose," he said, "but quickly. I shall count to three and if you have not chosen by then, I shall kill both of them."

He had put them on the ground, holding both of them with one hand. With the other hand he took out his pistol. He was counting: "One, two . . ."

"Here," she screamed. "That one!"

The explosive retort of the gun sounded in her ear.

And then she fainted dead away.

Rate this person's psychological pain (psychache) from 1 (least) to 9 (the highest imaginable). Circle one number:

1	2	3	4	5	6	7	8	⑨

Now think of the worst mental pain that *you* have ever experienced in your life. Keeping in mind the desciption of the terrible incident described above (as a kind of reference point), rate the worst psychache of your own life. Circle one number:

1	2	3	4	5	6	7	⑧	9

Check one, below:

____ My worst pain cannot be said to be in the same league as hers.

____ It is nowhere near what she describes.

____ It is not nearly as bad as what she describes.

__X__ It is not quite as bad; a shade less than what she describes.

____ It is as bad as what she describes.

____ It is even worse than what she describes.

My psychological pain related mostly to my *feelings* of (check three):

(X) abandonment   ( ) fear   ( ) powerlessness

( ) anger   ( ) grief   ( ) rejection

( ) anguish   (X) helplessness   ( ) sadness

( ) anxiety   ( ) hopelessness   (X) self-hate

( ) confusion   ( ) horror   ( ) shame

( ) despair   ( ) inadequacy   ( ) terror

( ) emptiness   ( ) jealousy   ( ) worthlessness

( ) failure   ( ) loneliness   ( ) OTHER: _____

My worst psychological pain related mostly to my *needs*° (check three):

(   ) to achieve difficult goals

(   ) to be loved by someone

(   ) to belong or to be affiliated

(   ) to overcome opposition

(   ) to be free of social confinement

(   ) to make up for past failure

(   ) to defend myself against others

(   ) to influence and control others

(   ) to receive attention from others

(   ) to avoid pain or injury

(   ) to avoid shame or humiliation

(   ) to protect my psychological space

(   ) to nurture or take care of someone

(   ) to keep things or ideas in good order

(   ) to enjoy sensuous experiences

(**X**) to be taken care of by someone

(**X**) to understand certain hows and whys

(**X**) OTHER: to   <u>be safe</u>

°Adapted from Henry A. Murray, *Explorations in Personality* (New York: Oxford University Press, 1938).

Please describe what your most intense psychological pain was: the circumstances, the incident, your situation in life, and the exact nature of the psychological pain as you experienced it.

At age 16, I experienced an undescribeble pain in my heart + mind. I did not want to live with this intense pain. It felt like a huge monster had taken me over, the pain was bigger than me. I was so small, I was drowning in pain. I did not understand. I felt crazy and isolated. I imagined spending the rest of my life in such pain and could not bear it. I refused to live in such suffering. People around me didn't notice. Everything just went about its business. The world didn't stop. No one did anything. I could not handle that. There was no way I could just go about living, acting out the "motions of life" in a complete trance. No one can live like that. Suicide was a relief.

Please describe what you did about that pain. Did you think about suicide? Attempt suicide? What were the actions in your life that were related to that pain? How did it finally resolve itself? Or, has it? Can you, in words, give some quantitative evaluation of that pain? What metaphors might you use to describe that pain?

I tried to kill myself. I took pills. I stabbed myself. I screamed for someone else to come stab me. I sat for long hours with a gun in my hand. I wrote a will, I imagined my own funeral, I cut on myself, hit myself, tried to starve myself to death, and finally I slashed the vein on my wrists open and bled. I remember watching the Life Blood flow out of me and feeling so relieved and finally relaxed. It was over at last.

Thank you for cooperating.

APPENDIX B

A Partial Listing of the Murray Psychological Needs*

Abasement   The need to submit passively to external force; to accept injury, blame, criticism, punishment; to surrender; to become resigned to fate; to admit inferiority, error, wrongdoing, or defeat; to confess and atone; to blame, belittle, or mutilate the self; to seek and enjoy pain, punishment, illness, and misfortune.

Achievement   The need to accomplish something difficult; to master, manipulate, or organize physical objects, human beings, or ideas; to do this as rapidly and independently as possible; to overcome obstacles and attain a high standard; to excel oneself; to rival and surpass others; to increase self-regard by the successful exercise of talent.

Affiliation   The need to draw near and enjoyably cooperate or reciprocate with an allied person (who likes the person); to please and win affection of the admired person; to adhere and remain loyal to a friend.

*Note: These descriptions are abstracts of the detailed explications of these needs in Henry A. Murray's *Explorations in Personality* (New York: Oxford University Press, 1938).

Aggression   The need to overcome opposition; to fight, attack, or injure another; to oppose forcefully or injure another; to belittle, censure, ridicule, slander; to be angry and rageful, combative, belligerent.

Autonomy   The need to get free, shake off restraint, break out of social confinement; to resist coercion and constriction; to avoid or quit activities prescribed by domineering authorities; to be independent and free and act according to desire; to defy convention.

Counteraction   The need to master or make up for failure by restriving; to obliterate a past humiliation by resumed action; to overcome weakiness; to repress fear; to effect a dishonor by action; to seek for obstacles and difficulties to overcome; to maintain self-respect and pride on a high level.

Defendance   The need to defend the self against assault, criticism, blame; to conceal or justify a misdeed, failure, or humiliation; to vindicate the ego.

Deference   The need to admire and support a superior; to praise, honor, or eulogize another; to yield eagerly to the influence of an allied other; to emulate an exemplar; to conform to custom.

Dominance   The need to control one's human environment; to influence or direct the behavior of others by suggestion, seduction, persuasion, or command; to dissuade, restrain, or prohibit.

Exhibition   The need to make an impression; to be seen and heard; to excite, amaze, fascinate, entertain, shock, intrigue, amuse, or entice others.

Harmavoidance   The need to avoid pain, physical injury, illness, and death; to escape from a dangerous situation; to take reasonable precautionary measures.

Inviolacy   The need to protect the self; to remain separate; to resist attempts by others to intrude on or invade one's own psychological space; to maintain a distance or separateness; to be isolated, immune from criticism.

Nurturance The need to *give* sympathy and gratify the needs of another person, especially someone who is weak (an infant), disabled, tired, inexperienced, infirm, defeated, lonely, humiliated, rejected, sick, mentally confused; to feed, help, support, console, protect, comfort, nurse, or heal; to nurture.

Order The need to put things or ideas in order; to achieve arrange, organize, balance, tidy, and work for precision among things in the outer world or ideas in the inner world.

Play The need to act for "fun" without further purpose; to laugh and make jokes; to have relaxation of stress; to participate in pleasurable activities for their own sake.

Rejection The need to separate oneself from negatively viewed persons; to exclude, abandon, expel, or remain indifferent to an inferior person; to snub or jilt another.

Sentience The need to seek sensuous experience; to give an important place to the creature comforts of taste and touch and the other senses; to enjoy good food and wine, silk sheets, expensive clothes.

Shame-avoidance The need to avoid humiliation and embarrassment; to avoid conditions that lead to scorn, derision, or indifference of others; to refrain from action because of fear of failure.

Succorance The need to *receive* support, help, and love; to have one's needs gratified by the sympathethic aid of another person; to be nursed, supported, sustained, protected, loved, guided, indulged, forgiven, consoled, taken care of.

Understanding The need to ask and answer questions; to speculate, formulate, analyze, and generalize; to want to know the answers to general questions; to theorize; to philosophize; to be curious; to want to know.

sanctuary see p 68

INDEX